P9-CAL-918

SCIENCE WORKSHOP SERIES
PHYSICAL SCIENCE
Chemical Changes

Seymour Rosen

This book is the
property of the
ELM ST. JR. HIGH SCHOOL

GLOBE BOOK COMPANY
A Division of Simon & Schuster
Englewood Cliffs, New Jersey

THE AUTHOR

Seymour Rosen received his B.A. and M.S. degrees from Brooklyn College. He taught science in the New York City School System for twenty-seven years. Mr. Rosen was also a contributing participant in a teacher-training program for the development of science curriculum for the New York City Board of Education.

Cover Photograph: Richard Menga, Fundamental Photographs
Photo Researcher: Rhoda Sidney

Photo Credits:

p. 3, Fig. G: Bethlehem Steel
p. 4, Fig. H: Cunard Lines
p. 4, Fig. I: General Motors
p. 4, Fig. J: Bayer/Monkmeyer Press
p. 14, Fig. K: Mimi Forsyth/Monkmeyer Press
p. 14, Fig. L: Mimi Forsyth/Monkmeyer Press
p. 32, Fig. C: NASA
p. 70, Fig. G: William Frost
p. 71, Fig. H: UPI
p. 80: Hugh Rogers/Monkmeyer Press
p. 94: The Image Works Archives
p. 124: Michael Kagan/Monkmeyer Press
p. 136, Fig. F: Gary Walts/The Image Works
p. 146, Fig. B: Gerard Fritz/Monkmeyer Press
p. 146, Fig. C: Rhoda Sidney
p. 152, Fig. C: Rhoda Sidney
p. 152, Fig. D: Arlene Collins/Monkmeyer Press
p. 152, Fig. E: Fredrik D. Bodin/Stock Boston
p. 152, Fig. F: Grant Heilman
p. 182, Fig. A: Helena Frost
p. 202, Fig. I: Department of Energy
p. 223, Fig. A: Helena Frost
p. 223, Fig. B: Helena Frost
p. 228: Bob Daemmrich/The Image Works

ISBN: 0-8359-0284-6

Copyright © 1992 by Globe Book Company, 190 Sylvan Avenue, Englewood Cliffs, New Jersey 07632. All rights reserved. No part of this book maybe kept in an information storage or retrieval system, transmitted or reproduced in any form or by any means without the prior written permission of the publisher.

Printed in the United States of America
1 2 3 4 5 6 7 8 9 10   95   94   93   92   91

Globe Book Company
A Division of Simon & Schuster
Englewood Cliffs, New Jersey

CONTENTS

Introduction to Chemical Changes

"Things change." "People change." "The more things change the more they stay the same."

You have heard these phrases. You probably have even used them yourself. People spend a lot of time talking about changes. You say "What's new?" when you see a friend. Every night on television, there are news programs to tell you what has happened that day.

Changes are what keeps life from being boring. If everything was exactly the same all the time, nothing would happen.

Fortunately, things do change. When they do, we need to understand the changes so we can change as well.

Scientists, like everyone else, are interested in changes. They study changes. They try to figure out how changes occur and why they happen.

This book is about chemical changes. Read it and you will understand a little bit more about the world around you. And you will be ready for the changes.

What is heat?

friction: force that opposes the motion of an object
heat: form of energy in moving particles of matter

LESSON 1 | What is heat?

Here is a trick question—Does an ice cube have heat? Think carefully! The answer is YES! An ice cube does have heat. It has <u>less</u> heat than water does, but is still has heat. All matter has heat. Some kinds of matter have more heat than other kinds.

WHAT IS HEAT?

Heat is a form of energy.

Heat is the energy of vibrating molecules — and molecules are always vibrating. This means that all matter has heat.

How hot an object is depends on how fast its molecules vibrate. The faster the molecules vibrate, the hotter the object is.

WHERE DOES HEAT COME FROM?

The sun provides most of our heat. The sun warms our earth. It makes plants and trees grow. Without the sun, we would have no food. And we need food to live.

Burning fuel provides some heat. Coal, oil, gas, and wood are some fuels that we burn. But without the sun, these fuels would not have formed.

Rubbing—or **friction**—also provides heat. Most heat that comes from friction is not wanted. For example, heat from friction can ruin machinery. Oil and grease help reduce friction.

Figure A *Molecules are always vibrating.*

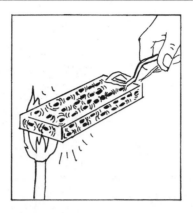

Figure B *Heat makes molecules vibrate faster.*

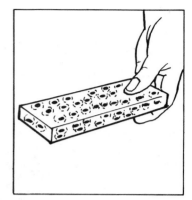

Figure C *When matter cools, its molecules vibrate more slowly.*

SOURCES OF HEAT

Figure D *The sun*

Figure E *Burning fuel*

Figure F *Friction*

Figure G

Nuclear reactions can give off a tremendous amount of heat. We are just learning how to use this heat.

In nuclear power plants, certain kinds of atoms are split. They give up energy in the form of heat. This heat changes water to steam. The steam turns the coils in generators, which produce electricity.

There are many kinds of energy. Heat is one kind of energy. Heat can make things move.

Figure H

Figure I

Heat moves ocean liners, diesel trucks—even your family car.

How does this happen?

1. Ocean liners, diesel trucks, and automobile engines burn fuel.
2. Fuel has stored chemical energy. The chemical energy changes to heat energy.
3. The high temperature causes great pressure.
4. The force of the pressure is used to move the vehicle.

Figure J

Heat has thousands of other uses too. For example, we use heat to warm our homes and to cook our food. Doctors use heat to kill germs. Heat is used to make metal products.

FILL IN THE BLANK

Complete each statement using a term or terms from the list below. Write your answers in the spaces provided. Some words may be used more than once.

energy	more	vibrating molecules
sun	move	heat
vibrating	friction	less

1. Energy can make things _____ .

2. Heat is a form of _____ .

3. Heat is caused by _____ .

4. All matter has _____ because molecules are always

   _____ .

5. Warm matter has _____ heat than cold matter.

6. Cool matter has _____ heat than warm matter.

7. The faster molecules vibrate, the _____ heat they give off.

8. The slower molecules vibrate, the _____ heat they give off.

9. Most heat comes from the _____ .

10. Rubbing produces heat. Another name for rubbing is _____ .

MATCHING

Match each term in Column A with its description in Column B. Write the correct letter in the space provided.

	Column A		Column B
_____	1. friction	a)	gives us most of our heat
_____	2. sun	b)	examples of fuel
_____	3. vibrating molecules	c)	can make things move
_____	4. energy	d)	rubbing
_____	5. coal, wood, oil, gas	e)	cause all heat

TRUE OR FALSE

In the space provided, write "true" if the sentence is true. Write "false" if the sentence is false.

_____ 1. All molecules vibrate.

_____ 2. Molecules always vibrate at the same speed.

_____ 3. The faster molecules vibrate, the less heat they give off.

_____ 4. Most of our heat comes from the moon.

_____ 5. Coal, wood, oil, and gas are fuels.

_____ 6. Without the sun, we would have no coal, wood, oil, or gas.

_____ 7. A piece of dust has heat.

_____ 8. A flame always give off heat.

_____ 9. Heat always give off a flame.

_____ 10. Heat can do work.

WORD SCRAMBLE

Below are several scrambled words you have used in this Lesson. Unscramble the words and write your answers in the spaces provided.

1. REGYEN   _____

2. LUFE   _____

3. TROCINIF   _____

4. TEAH   _____

5. BUNGBIR   _____

How does heat change the size of matter?

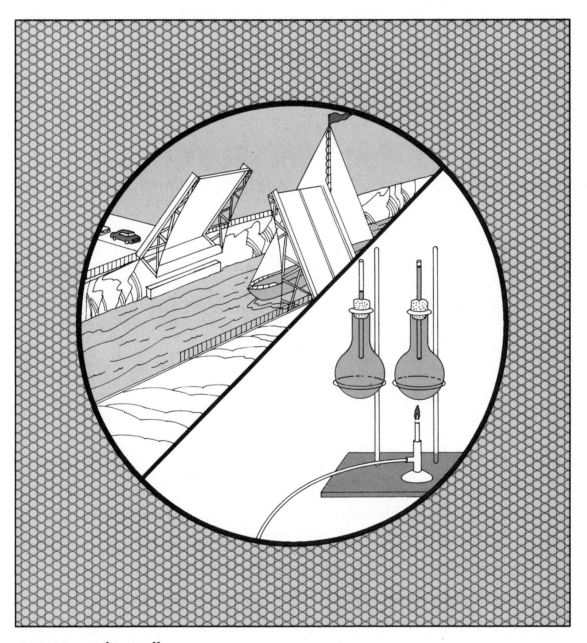

contract: make smaller
expand: make larger

LESSON 2 | How does heat change the size of matter?

Household hint: If you cannot open the lid of a jar, hold the lid under hot water. Then unsecure the lid. Why does hot water work? The heat makes the lid a tiny bit <u>larger</u>. Then it is easier to turn.

HEAT MAKES THINGS LARGER.

As you know, matter is made up of atoms and molecules. And they are always vibrating. The greater the heat, the faster they vibrate. When molecules vibrate faster, they need more room. They make more room by s–p–r–e–a–d–i–n–g o–u–t. The heated matter becomes larger. It **expands**.

When matter cools, the opposite happens. The molecules vibrate slower. Now they need less room. They move closer together. This makes the matter smaller. It **contracts**.

Most matter:

- expands when heated.

- contracts when cooled.

Temperature is always changing—becoming warmer or cooler. The size of matter is always changing, too. Usually, matter expands or contracts only slightly. Sometimes, size changes very little. Then it is not important. Other times, size changes a lot. Then it is very important. For example, when heat expands a roadway, the roadway can buckle. Heat expansion can make drawbridges stick.

Different kinds of matter expand at different rates. Some matter expands a great deal. Other matter expands only a little.

HOW DO HEAT AND COLD CHANGE THE SIZE OF A SOLID?

What You Need (Materials)

brass ring
brass ball that "just" fits through the ring
Bunsen burner
cold water

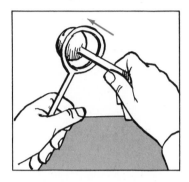

Figure A

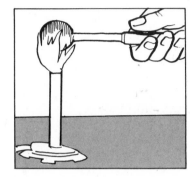

Figure B

Figure C

How To Do the Experiment

1. Pass the brass ball through the ring. Notice the close fit (Figure A).

2. Heat the ball over the flame for about one minute (Figure B).

3. Now try to pass the ball through the ring (Figure C).

What You Learned (Observations)

4. The heated ball _____ pass through the ring.
   did, did not

5. The heat made the ball _____ .
   smaller, larger

6. The ball _____ .
   expanded, contracted

Next Steps

cold water

Figure D

Figure E

7. Dip the heated ball into the cold water (Figure D).

8. Try to pass the ball through the ring (Figure E).

What You Learned (Observations)

9. After the ball cooled, it _____ pass through the ring.
   did, did not

10. The cold water made the ball _____ .
    smaller, larger

11. The ball _____ .
    expanded, contracted

Something To Think About (Conclusions)

12. Heat _____ a solid.
    expands, contracts

13. Cold _____ a solid.
    expands, contracts

MATCHING

Match each term in Column A with its description in Column B. Write the correct letter in the space provided.

	Column A	Column B
_____	1. molecules	a) makes molecules vibrate faster
_____	2. heat	b) sun
_____	3. cold	c) always vibrating
_____	4. states of matter	d) solids, liquids, gases
_____	5. source of most heat	e) makes molecules vibrate slower
_____	6. expand	f) to make smaller
_____	7. contract	g) expand when heated
_____	8. solids	h) to make larger

HOW DO HEAT AND COLD CHANGE THE SIZE OF A LIQUID?

What You Need (Materials)

Pyrex bottle
cold, colored water
one-holed stopper with glass tube
warm water
large beaker

Figure F

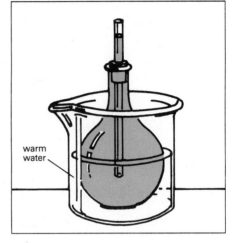

warm water

Figure G

How To Do the Experiment (Procedure)

1. Put cold, colored water in the bottle. Cap the bottle with the one-holed stopper. Put a glass tube through the hold of the stopper and into the water (Figure F).

2. Heat the bottle gently by placing it in a warm-water bath (Figure G). Then take the bottle out of the warm water. [Watch the water level in the tube].

What You Learned (Observations)

3. When you heated the bottle, the water in the tube moved _____ .
   _{up, down}

4. The water rose because it _____ .
   _{expanded, contracted}

5. When you took away the heat, the water became _____ .
   _{cooler, warmer}

6. The water moved _____ in the tube.
   _{up, down}

7. The water moved down because it _____ .
   _{expanded, contracted}

Something To Think About (Conclusions)

8. When a liquid is heated it _____ .
   _{expands, contracts}

9. When a liquid cools, it _____ .
   _{expands, contracts}

HOW DO HEAT AND COLD CHANGE THE SIZE OF GAS?

What You Need (Materials)

Pyrex bottle
cold colored water
one-holed stopper
with bulb glass tube

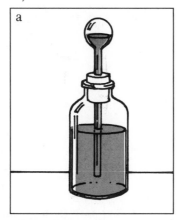

Figure H

Figure I

How To Do The Experiment (Procedure)

1. Set up the equipment as shown (Figure H).

2. Heat the bulb gently by wrapping your hands around it (Figure I). Keep your hands around the bulb for at least one minute. Then take your hands away. Watch the water level in the tube.

What You Learned (Observations)

3. There is mostly _____ in the bulb.
   _{water, gas}

4. When you heated the bulb, the gas took up _____ room.
   _{more, less}

5. The gas _____ .
   _{expanded, contracted}

6. The expanded gas made the water in the tube _____ .
   _{rise, move down}

7. When you took away the heat, the gas _____ .
   _{became warmer, became cooler}

8. The gas _____ .
   _{expanded, contracted}

9. The gas pressed on the water with _____ force.
   _{more, less}

10. The water in the tube moved _____ .
    _{up, down}

Something To Think About (Conclusions)

11. When a gas is heated, it _____ .
    _{expands, contracts}

12. When a gas cools, it _____ .
    _{expands, contracts}

12

EXCEPTIONS

Figure J

You have learned that matter expands when heated and contracts when cooled. But there are <u>exceptions</u>.

For example, water contracts as its temperature drops. BUT when it changes to solid ice, it expands.

FILL IN THE BLANK

Complete each statement using a term or terms from the list below. Write your answers in the spaces provided. Some words may be used more than once.

expand	heated	more
contracts	become smaller	become larger
heat	less	vibrating

1. Most matter expands when _____ .

2. Molecules are always _____ .

3. Vibrating molecules give off _____ .

4. When molecules vibrate faster, they give off _____ heat.

5. When molecules vibrate faster, they need _____ room.

6. Heat makes matter _____ in size.
   (one word)

7. When molecules vibrate slower, they give off _____ heat.

8. When molecules vibrate slower, they need _____ room.

9. Matter that cools _____ in size.
   (one word)

10. Expand means _____ ; contract means _____ .

TRUE OR FALSE

In the space provided, write "true" if the sentence is true. Write "false" if the sentence is false.

_____ 1. All molecules vibrate.

_____ 2. The slower molecules vibrate, the more heat they give off.

_____ 3. Matter contracts when it is heated.

_____ 4. Matter contracts when it is cooled.

_____ 5. All matter expands and contracts the same amount.

_____ 6. When matter expands, it takes up less room.

_____ 7. When matter contracts, it takes up more room.

_____ 8. Liquid water expands as it changes to ice.

_____ 9. All matter expands as it cools.

_____ 10. Some matter expands only a little when it is heated.

REACHING OUT

Figure J

Figure K

1. Why do overhead wires hang with a slight sag in the summertime? _____

_____

2. Why do the same wires hang tightly during the wintertime? _____

_____

14

How does heat move through solids?

3

conduction [kun-DUK-shun]: way heat moves through solids
conductors: substances that conduct heat easily
insulators: substances that do not conduct heat easily

LESSON 3 | How does heat move through solids?

Did you ever grab a hot pan handle? The handle was hot even though it wasn't over the burner. How did the heat move to the handle?

First, the bottom of the pan became hot. The molecules there vibrated faster and faster. As they vibrated, they bumped into other molecules. Then, the other molecules became hot, vibrated faster, and bumped into other molecules.

This happened over and over again. As it did, the heat moved farther along. Soon, the entire pan was hot.

The passing along of heat from molecule to molecule is called **conduction** [kun-DUK-shun]. Only solids move heat by conduction.

In solids, the molecules are packed very close together. They cannot move from place to place. The molecules just vibrate faster and faster when a solid is heated.

All solids conduct heat. Some conduct heat much better than others. Solids that conduct heat well are called good **conductors**. Metals are the best heat conductors.

Wood, glass, and plastics do not conduct heat well. They are poor conductors. Poor conductors are used as **insulators**. Insulators keep heat from moving where it is not wanted. They keep things from becoming too hot or too cold. If the handle of the pan is covered by an insulator, you won't burn your hand.

Insulators protect us from heat and cold. They keep us comfortable.

HOW CONDUCTION TAKES PLACE

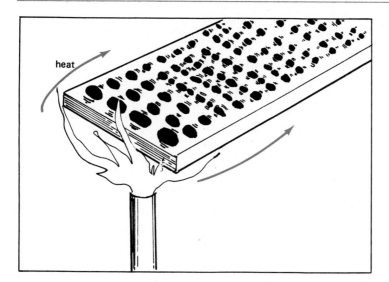

Figure A

Heat moves through solids by conduction.

In conduction, heat is passed along from molecule to molecule.

STUDYING CONDUCTION

Look at each picture. Then answer the questions for Figures B and C.

Figure B

Figure B shows six rings of wax on a metal rod. The flame has just been placed under the rod.

1. Which wax ring will melt first?

   _____

2. Which wax ring will melt last?

   _____

3. Which end gets hot first? _____

4. Which end gets hot last? _____

5. What do we call the way heat moves in

   solids? _____

17

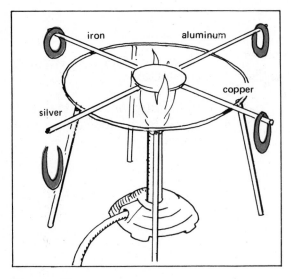

Figure C shows wax rings at same distance from flame.

6. Are all the wax rings melting at the same time? _____

7. Are the rods made of the same metal? _____

8. Which one of these rods is the best conductor of heat? _____

Figure C

9. You know that it is the best conductor of heat because the wax melted around it

   _____ .

   first, last

10. Which rod is the worst conductor of heat? _____

11. You know that it is the worst conductor of heat because the wax melts around it

    _____ .

    first, last

12. This experiment shows that conduction is _____ .

    the same for all solids, different for different solids

TRUE OR FALSE

In the space provided, write "true" if the sentence is true. Write "false" if the sentence is false.

_____ 1. All matter has heat.

_____ 2. Heat can move from place to place.

_____ 3. Molecules vibrate slower when they are heated.

_____ 4. Heat moves through liquids and gases by conduction.

_____ 5. Conduction moves heat from molecule to molecule.

_____ 6. In conduction, molecules move from place to place.

_____ 7. All solids are good conductors of heat.

_____ 8. Metals are good conductors of heat.

_____ 9. Metals are good insulators of heat.

_____ 10. Wood and plastics are good insulators of heat.

FILL IN THE BLANK

Complete each statement using a term or terms from the list below. Write your answers in the spaces provided.

insulator	faster	solids
vibrate	metals	heat
conduction	bump	do not
prevent	better	

1. Heat makes molecules vibrate _____ .

2. The faster molecules vibrate, the more they _____ into other molecules.

3. When molecules hit other molecules, the other molecules _____

   faster and give off more _____ .

4. The passing of heat from molecule to molecule is called _____ .

5. Only _____ move heat by conduction.

6. Molecules of solids _____ move from place to place.

7. The best conductors of heat are _____ .

8. Some metals are _____ heat conductors than others.

9. A poor conductor is called an _____ .

10. The job of an insulator is to _____ heat from being conducted.

MATCHING

Match each term in Column A with its description in Column B. Write the correct letter in the space provided.

	Column A	Column B
_____	1. insulate	a) good heat conductors
_____	2. metals	b) give off heat energy
_____	3. conduction	c) poor heat conductors
_____	4. plastics and wood	d) to prevent heat from being conducted
_____	5. vibrating molecules	e) the way heat moves in solids

WORD SEARCH

The list on the left contains words that you have used in this Lesson. Find and circle each word where it appears in the box. The spellings may go in any direction: up, down, left, right, or diagonally.

HEAT

SUN

FRICTION

ENERGY

FUEL

EXPAND

CONTRACT

T	E	N	D	R	H	F
C	X	O	N	E	O	X
A	P	I	A	N	L	A
R	L	T	P	O	E	N
T	S	C	X	N	U	H
N	O	I	E	S	F	L
O	P	R	I	R	T	N
C	G	F	F	I	C	O
Y	G	I	O	L	F	U

REACHING OUT

An iron pot and a copper pot are the same size and shape. Both pots are heated.

1. Which pot will heat up faster? _____

Both pots are heated to the same temperature and allowed to cool.

2. Which pot will cool faster? _____

How does heat move through liquids and gases?

4

convection [kuhn-VEK-shun]:   way heat moves through liquids and gases

LESSON 4 | How does heat move through liquids and gases?

You have learned that the molecules of solids are packed very close together. When a solid is heated, its molecules vibrate faster, but they <u>cannot</u> move from place to place.

The molecules of liquids and gases are <u>not</u> tightly packed. There are spaces between the molecules. This means that the molecules <u>can</u> move from place to place.

What happens when a liquid or gas is heated?

- The molecules closest to the heat get hot first. They vibrate faster. They also move. They move away from the heat.

- Cooler molecules move in and take their place.

- The cooler molecules are heated. Then they move away.

- Other molecules move in to take their place.

This happens over and over again. Little by little, all the molecules in the gas or liquid are heated. The molecules that were heated first cool a bit. Then they move back toward the heat and are heated again. This happens over and over—heating, cooling, and then re-heating.

The passing along of heat by moving molecules is called **convection** [kuhn-VEK-shun]. Only gases and liquids are heated by convection.

WHAT DO THE DIAGRAMS SHOW?

The diagrams below show atoms of solids, liquids, and gases. Study the diagrams. Then answer the questions below.

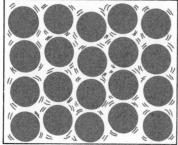

Figure A *Atoms of solids*

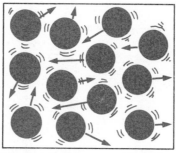

Figure B *Atoms of liquids*

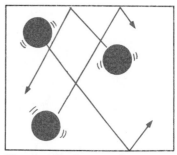

Figure C *Atoms of gases*

Which atoms . . .

1. are closest together? _____

2. are farthest apart? _____

3. vibrate? _____

4. do not vibrate? _____

5. do not move from place to place? _____

6. move from place to place? _____

7. move the most? _____

8. become hot by conduction? _____

9. become hot by convection? _____

STUDYING CONVECTION IN A LIQUID

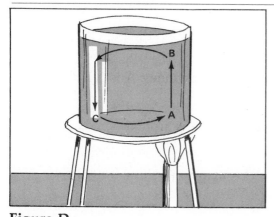

Figure D

1. The water at A is heated first. It rises to B.

2. As it rises, it cools a bit.

3. The cooled water turns around and drops to C. Then it moves to A again. Here it is reheated.

4. Now, start again with Step 1. Repeat the steps over and over and over again.

Figure E

1. The sun heats the air. The air over the ground at A becomes warm first. It rises to B.

2. As it rises, it cools.

3. The cooler air turns around and drops to C. Then it moves to A again. Here it is reheated.

4. Now start again with Step 1. Repeat the steps over and over again.

When the air from A rises, other air from C moves in to take its place. What do you call

this kind of moving air?_____ (Take a guess. You know this term and use it often.)

This is called a convection box. The burning candle makes air move out of one chimney and into the other.

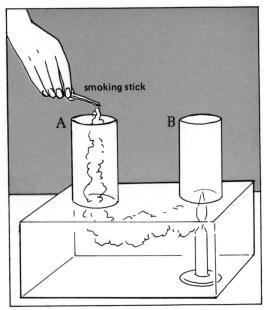

Figure F

1. Which air is warmer? The air in

   chimney ——————————— .

                          A,B

2. Which air is cooler? The air in

   chimney ——————————— .

                          A,B

3. Air in chimney B is ——————————.

                                   rising, falling

4. The air in chimney A is ——————————.

                                   rising, falling

5. Air is moving from ——————————— .

                               A to B, B to A

6. Draw arrows to show how the air moves.

FILL IN THE BLANK

Complete each statement using a term or terms from the list below. Write your answers in the spaces provided.

take their place	conduction	gases
convection	more	friction
cannot	solids	vibrating
sun	move away	

1. Molecules of _____ are closest together.

2. Molecules of _____ are farthest apart.

3. Heat moves through solids by a method called _____ .

4. Heat moves through liquids and gases by a method called _____ .

5. Heat is caused by _____ molecules.

6. The faster molecules vibrate, the _____ heat they give off.

7. In conduction, vibrating molecules_____ move from place to place.

8. In convection, heated molecules _____ and other molecules

   _____ .

9. Almost all of our heat energy comes from the _____ .

10. Another name for rubbing is _____ .

MATCHING

Match each term in Column A with its description in Column B. Write the correct letter in the space provided.

Column A	Column B
_____ 1. conduction	a) molecules farthest apart
_____ 2. convection	b) the way heat moves through solids
_____ 3. solids	c) source of most of our energy
_____ 4. gases	d) the way heat moves through liquids and gases
_____ 5. sun	e) molecules closest together

TRUE OR FALSE

In the space provided, write "true" if the sentence is true. Write "false" if the sentence is false.

_____ 1. Only molecules of solids vibrate.

_____ 2. Molecules of solids can move from place to place.

_____ 3. Molecules of liquids and gases can move from place to place.

_____ 4. Molecules of liquids are closer together than molecules of gases.

_____ 5. Molecules of solids are closer together than molecules of liquids.

_____ 6. Heat makes molecules vibrate faster.

_____ 7. The faster molecules vibrate, the more heat they give off.

_____ 8. Cooling makes molecules vibrate faster.

_____ 9. All molecules vibrate at the same speed.

_____ 10. The sun heats the earth.

REACHING OUT

Why should a window be opened from the top <u>and</u> the bottom?

_____

_____

_____

_____

_____

How does heat move through empty space?

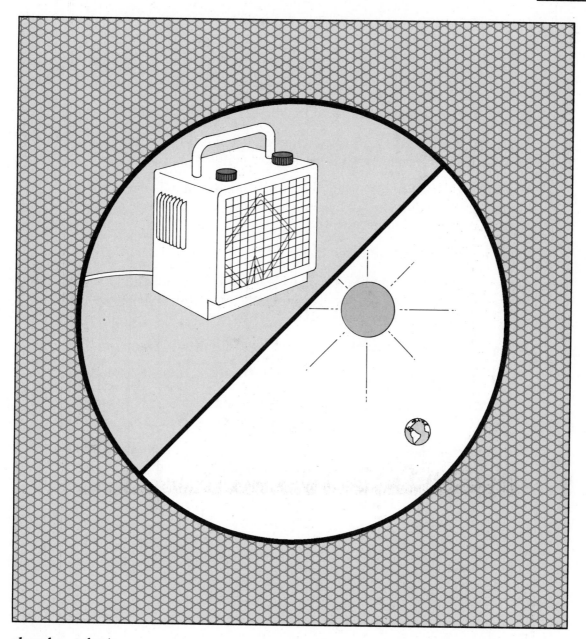

absorb: take in
radiation [ray-dee-AY-shun]: the way heat moves through empty space
reflect: bounce off

LESSON 5 | How does heat move through empty space?

Can heat move where there is no matter?

You have learned that with conduction and convection, heat is carried by vibrating molecules. And molecules are matter.

Most of our heat comes from the sun. And the sun is 150 million kilometers (93 million miles) away. Most of this great distance is empty space. There are no molecules there.

Then, how does the heat reach us?

There is a third way that heat travels. Heat moves through empty space by **radiation** [ray-dee-AY-shun]. Radiation needs no molecules. The sun's heat reaches us by radiation.

When the sun's heat reaches the earth, two things happen.

- Part of the heat bounces off the surface of the earth. It is **reflected**.

- Part of the heat is taken in by the air, water, and land. It is **absorbed**. Matter warms up when it absorbs heat energy.

Radiation does not come only from outer space. Heat from a flame or a hot object reaches us by radiation. We would feel some of the heat even if there were no molecules of air around us.

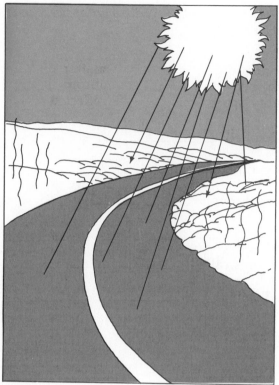

Figure A *Dark colors absorb heat.*

Figure B *Light colors reflect heat.*

1. This means that...

   a) dark colors _____ than light colors.
   become warmer, stay cooler

   b) light colors _____ than dark colors.
   become warmer, stay cooler

2. In the winter, _____ colored clothing helps keep us warm.
   light, dark

3. In the summer, _____ colored clothing helps keep us cool.
   light, dark

4. Would you wear dark colored clothing or light colored clothing if you lived near a desert or near the equator?

   _____

5. Would you wear dark colored clothing or light colored clothing if you lived in the far north or far south?

   _____

Complete each statement using a term or terms from the list below. Write your answers in the spaces provided. Some words may be used more than once.

<table>
<tr><td>reflect</td><td>conduction</td><td>matter</td></tr>
<tr><td>radiation</td><td>absorbed</td><td>absorb</td></tr>
<tr><td>convection</td><td>empty space</td><td>reflected</td></tr>
</table>

1. Heat moves through solids by a method called _____ .

2. Heat moves through liquids and gases by a method called _____ .

3. In conduction and convection, heat moves through _____ .

4. Between the sun and the earth there is mostly _____ .

5. Energy that can move through empty space is called _____ .

6. The sun's energy reaches us by a method called _____ .

7. Energy that is taken in is "_____ ."

8. Energy that bounces off is "_____ ."

9. Dark colors _____ heat.

10. Light colors _____ heat.

CONDUCTION, CONVECTION, OR RADIATION?

Fill in each blank space with one or more of these terms.

1. The way heat moves through liquids and gases. _____

2. The way heat reaches the moon. _____

3. The way heat moves through solids. _____

4. Heat-movement that needs no molecules. _____

5. Heat-movements that need molecules. _____ _____

COMPLETING SENTENCES

Choose the correct word or term for each statement. Write your choice in the spaces provided.

1. Heat moves through solids by _____.
   conduction, convection, radiation

2. Heat moves through liquids by _____.
   conduction, convection, radiation

3. Heat moves through gases by _____.
   conduction, convection, radiation

4. Heat moves through empty space by _____.
   conduction, convection, radiation

5. Conduction_____ need molecules.
   does, does not

6. Convection _____ need molecules.
   does, does not

7. Radiation _____ need molecules.
   does, does not

8. Heat that reaches the earth is _____.
   absorbed only, reflected only, absorbed or reflected

9. Dark colors _____ more heat than light colors.
   absorb, reflect

10. Light colors _____ more than dark colors
    absorb, reflect

WORD SCRAMBLE

Below are several scrambled words you have used in this Lesson. Unscramble the words and write your answers in the spaces provided.

1. DAITRONIA _____

2. CONCONUTDIN _____

3. BRASBO _____

4. FLERTCE _____

5. TONICVECON _____

MATCHING

Match each term in Column A with its description in Column B. Write the correct letter in the space provided.

Column A

_____ 1. conduction and convection

_____ 2. radiation

_____ 3. dark colors

_____ 4. light colors

_____ 5. molecules

Column B

a)   absorb radiation

b)   always vibrating

c)   need molecules

d)   reflect radiation

e)   needs no molecules

REACHING OUT

Figure C

Objects in space are constantly being heated by the sun. These objects are covered with reflective materials to protect them from the heat of the sun.

Which will absorb less heat; a light colored object or a cover with reflective materials.

Why? _____

_____

What is the difference between heat and temperature?

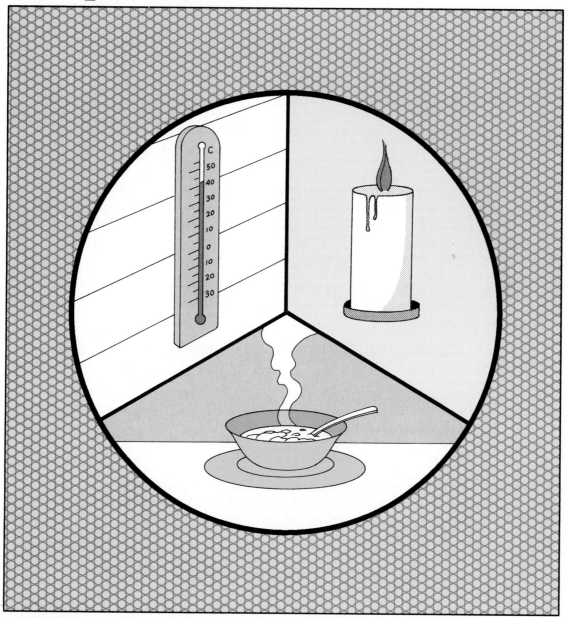

calorie [KAL-uh-ree]: unit used to measure heat
degree: unit used to measure temperature
temperature: measure of how hot or cold something is
thermometer: instrument to measure temperature

LESSON 6 | What is the difference between heat and temperature?

"What a hot day!"

"Gee! It's cold!"

"What's the temperature outside?"

"Ma! My head feels warm!"

We often talk about heat and temperature. Are they the same?

Heat and temperature are <u>related</u>. But they are <u>not</u> the same.

TEMPERATURE   The word **temperature** is used to describe the amount of heat felt. Temperature is measured with a **thermometer**. Temperature is measured in **degrees**. We use different thermometers to measure the temperatures of our bodies, the temperature outdoors, the temperature of an oven. But the measurement is always in degrees.

Temperature depends on how fast molecules vibrate. The faster molecules vibrate, the higher the temperature. The slower they vibrate, the lower the temperature.

HEAT   Heat is the total energy given off by all the vibrating molecules in a bit of matter.

Heat depends on two things:

• How fast molecules vibrate (temperature).

• How many molecules vibrate.

This means that size affects the amount of heat. Larger things have more molecules. So if you have a large object and a small object that both have the same temperature, the large object will have more heat.

Heat is measured in **calories** [KAL-uh-reez]. Have you heard that word before?

Test your understanding of temperature and heat. Study the figure below. Then answer the questions.

boiling water

Figure A

Look at Figure A. Both the match and the water are hot. The flame has a higher temperature than boiling water.

1. Can a single match boil this much water? _____

2. Which one do you think can melt more ice? _____
   <small>the burning match, the boiling water</small>

3. Which has more heat? _____
   <small>the burning match, the boiling water</small>

4. This shows that higher temperature _____ always mean more heat.
   <small>does, does not</small>

5. The boiling water has more heat because it has _____ .
   <small>more molecules, a higher temperature</small>

6. The term that describes the "feeling" of heat is _____ .
   <small>calories, temperature</small>

7. The term that describes total heat energy is _____ .
   <small>calories, temperature</small>

Look at Figure B. Answer the following questions.

Figure B *Both pots contain boiling water.*

8. The temperature of pot a is _____ the temperature in
   pot b.
   <u>higher than, lower than, the same as</u>

9. The molecules in pot a are vibrating _____ the molecules
   in pot b.
   <u>more than, less than, at the same speed as</u>

10. Pot a and pot b _____ have the same number of calories.
    <u>do, do not</u>

11. _____ has fewer calories.
    <u>Pot a, Pot b</u>

12. _____ has more calories.
    <u>Pot a, Pot b</u>

FILL IN THE BLANK

Complete each statement using a term or terms from the list below. Write your answers in the spaces provided. Some words may be used more than once.

less heat
lower temperature
expand
how fast molecules vibrate

degrees
related
higher temperature
calories

not
the number of molecules
more heat

1. Heat and temperature are _____ but they are _____ the same.

2. Temperature depends upon _____.

3. Heat depends on _____ and also on _____ that vibrate.

4. Faster vibrating molecules mean a _____.

5. Slower vibrating molecules mean a _____.

6. More vibrating molecules usually mean _____.

7. Fewer vibrating molecules usually mean _____.

8. Temperature is measured in units called _____.

9. Heat is measured in units called _____ .

10. Heat makes matter _____ .

MATCHING

Match each term in Column A with its description in Column B. Write the correct letter in the space provided.

Column A

_____ 1. temperature

_____ 2. heat

_____ 3. degree

_____ 4. calorie

_____ 5. temperature and heat

Column B

a) depends upon how fast molecules vibrate and how many molecules vibrate

b) measure of heat

c) related but not the same

d) measure of temperature

e) depends upon how fast molecules vibrate

TRUE OR FALSE

In the space provided, write "true" if the sentence is true. Write "false" if the sentence is false.

_____   **1.** Heat comes from vibrating molecules.

_____   **2.** Molecules always vibrate at the same speed.

_____   **3.** The faster molecules vibrate, the less heat they give off.

_____   **4.** Temperature tells us how fast molecules vibrate.

_____   **5.** Temperature is measured in calories.

_____   **6.** We measure temperature with a barometer.

_____   **7.** Heat depends only on how fast molecules vibrate.

_____   **8.** Ice has heat.

_____   **9.** An ice cube has the same amount of heat as a block of ice.

_____   **10.** Heat energy is measured in calories.

REACHING OUT

Is it possible for something small which has a high temperature to have the same amount of heat as something large which has a low temperature?

_____

How does a thermometer work?

7

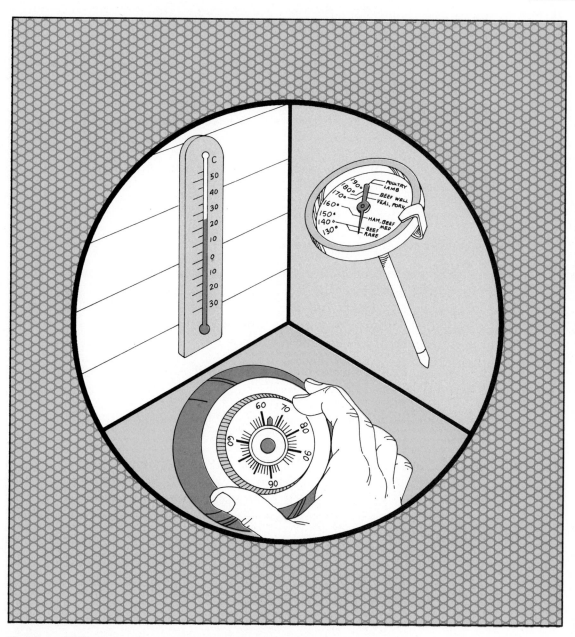

Celsius [SEL-see-us]:   metric temperature scale
Fahrenheit [FER-un-hyt]:   temperature scale

LESSON 7 | How does a thermometer work?

Think of all the ways you use thermometers. They tell you indoor temperature and outdoor temperature. A thermometer in meat tells whether your food is done. When you don't feel well, you take your temperature with a thermometer.

No matter what kind of thermometer you use, it works because of two facts you already know:

- Matter expands when it is heated.

- Matter contracts when it is cooled.

In most thermometers the matter that expands or contracts is a liquid. The main part of a thermometer is a long closed tube. At one end the tube gets larger. This end is called closed the bulb. The bulb is filled with a liquid that runs part way up the tube. In most thermometers, the liquid is either mercury or colored alcohol.

- When the liquid in a thermometer is heated, it expands. It rises in the tube.

- When the liquid in the thermometer is cooled, it contracts. It falls in the tube.

Numbers and lines on the side of the tube tell us the temperature in degrees. There are two popular temperature scales. In the United States, the **Fahrenheit** [FER-un-hyt] scale is often used. In most of the rest of the world, the **Celsius** [SEL-see-us] scale is used. Scientists everywhere use the Celsius scale.

STUDYING THERMOMETERS

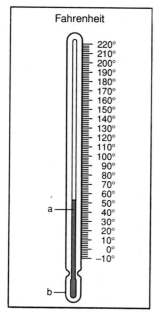

Figure A

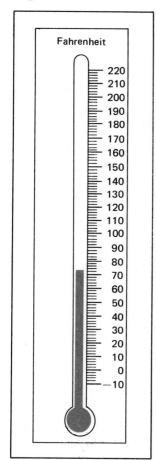

Figure B

Look at the thermometers in Figures A and B. Then answer the questions.

1. The tube is lettered _____ .

a, b

2. The bulb is lettered _____ .

a, b

3. Name two liquids that are used in liquid thermometers.

   _____

4. When heated, the liquid _____ in the tube.

rises, falls

5. When cooled, the liquid _____ in the tube.

rises, falls

6. This is a _____ scale thermometer.

Fahrenheit, Celsius

The temperature on this Fahrenheit thermometer is 72 degrees. In symbol form it is written 72° F.

7. How do you think you write 72 degrees Celsius?

   _____

8. In this thermometer, how many degrees does each line stand for? _____

9. Take a guess! Do all thermometers have the same number of degrees between lines? _____

10. Write the following temperatures in symbol form:

    a) twenty-two degrees Fahrenheit _____ .

    b) one hundred degrees Celsius _____ .

    c) minus five degrees Fahrenheit _____ .

    d) seventy-nine degrees Fahrenheit _____ .

    e) forty-four degrees Celsius _____ .

Some thermometers tell temperature because a metal coil inside them expands and contracts.

Oven and meat thermometers are examples. So are the thermometers in thermostats.

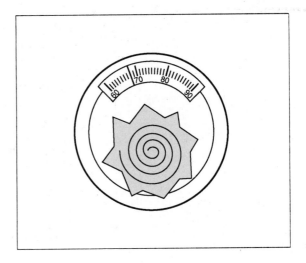

Figure C

FILL IN THE BLANK

Complete each statement using a term or terms from the list below. Write your answers in the spaces provided. Some answers may be used more than once.

become smaller	colored alcohol	become bigger
falls	liquid	heated
Fahrenheit	thermometer	mercury
cooled	rises	Celsius

1. We measure temperature with a _____ .

2. A thermometer works because matter expands when _____ and

   contracts when _____ .

3. There are two main kinds of temperature scales. They are _____ and

   _____ .

4. In science the _____ scale is used most often.

5. In most thermometers, a _____ is used.

6. Two common liquids used in thermometers are _____ and

   _____ .

7. When heated, the liquid _____ in the thermometer tube.

8. When cooled, the liquid _____ in the thermometer tube.

9. Contract means to _____ .

10. Expand means to _____ .

The diagram below shows a Fahrenheit thermometer and a Celsius thermometer.
See how the scales are different. Study them. Then fill in the temperatures below.
Line up the numbers with a straight edge. Each line stands for two degrees.

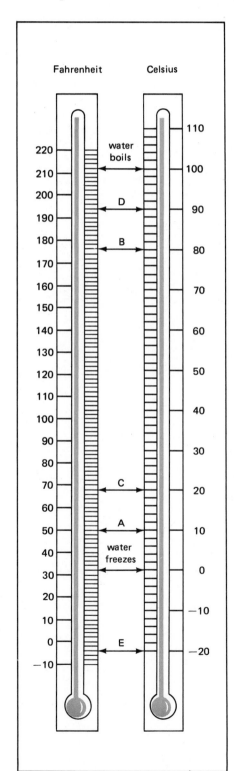

Fill in the missing information in the charts below.

		Fahrenheit	**Celsius**
1.	Water boils		
2.	Water Freezes		

	Point on Thermometers	**Fahrenheit**	**Celsius**
3.	A	50°	
4.	B		80°
5.	C		20°
6.	D	194°	
7.	E	−4°	

Now answer these questions.

8. 86° F is the same temperature as _____ °C.

9. 104° F is the same temperature as _____ °C.

10. 50° C is the same temperature as _____ °F.

11. −10° C is the same temperature as _____ °F.

12. 40° C is the same temperature as _____ °F.

13. 60° C is the same temperature as _____ °F.

14. 158° F is the same temperature as _____ °C.

15. What temperature would you want it to be all
the time? Write your answer in both Fahrenheit
and Celsius.

_____ °F

_____ °C

43

WORD SEARCH

The list on the left contains words that you have used in this Lesson. Find and circle each word where it appears in the box. The spellings may go in any direction: up, down, left, right, or diagonally.

LIQUID

CALORIE

VIBRATE

DEGREE

MATTER

ABSORB

REFLECT

B	R	O	S	B	A	Q	L
R	E	T	T	A	M	V	D
Q	F	S	A	P	I	P	E
L	L	T	I	B	S	O	L
D	E	G	R	E	E	L	F
I	C	A	O	L	M	I	E
P	T	D	I	U	Q	I	L
E	I	R	O	L	A	C	R

REACHING OUT

Why is water not used in thermometers? _____

_____

_____

_____

What are compounds and molecules?

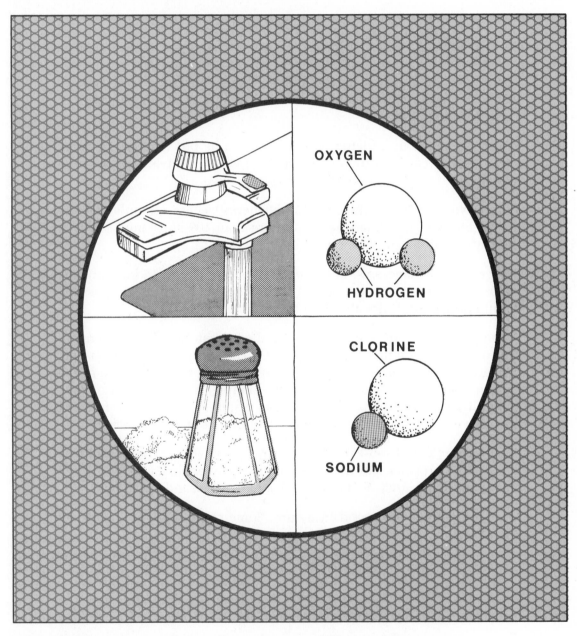

compound: matter made up of two or more different elements
molecule [MAHL-uh-kyool]:   the smallest part of a compound that has all the
   properties of that compound, two or more atoms linked together

LESSON 8 | What are compounds and molecules?

There are only 26 letters in the alphabet, but you know thousands of words. A good dictionary has hundreds of thousands of words in it. How this the possible?

Words are made up of letters and letters can be put together in many ways. Words can be different lengths. Most words use two or more letters. Some use the same letter more than once.

What if you combined the chemical elements? There are only 109 elements, but we <u>know</u> that there are more than 109 substances. In fact, there are millions and millions of substances.

Most of the substances we know are made up of two or more elements: water, salt, carbon dioxide, baking soda. These substances are possible because atoms of different elements can link up.

A **compound** is a substance made of linked-up atoms. The elements in the compound lose their own properties. The compound takes on new properties. Compounds do not even have to be in the same state as the elements of which they are made. For example, hydrogen and oxygen are both gases. They can link up to make water—a liquid. A compound must have at least one metal element and one nonmetal element.

A **molecule** [MAHL-uh-kyool] is the smallest part of a compound that still has the properties of that compound. A molecule has two or more atoms linked together. Some molecules have thousands of atoms.

Most compounds are found in nature. Some compounds are made by scientists.

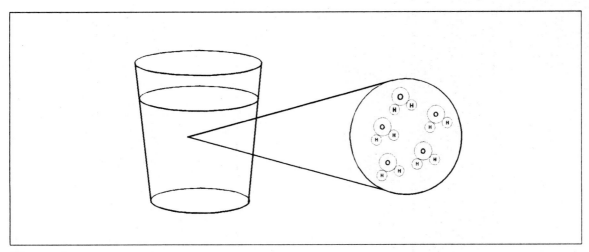

Figure A

Water is a liquid compound. A glass of water has billions and billions of water molecules in it. Each molecule is <u>exactly</u> <u>alike</u>. Each molecule has all of the properties of water. The smallest part of a compound is just <u>one</u> <u>molecule</u> of that compound.

Water is made up of the elements hydrogen and oxygen. Two hydrogen atoms and one oxygen atom combine to make one water molecule.

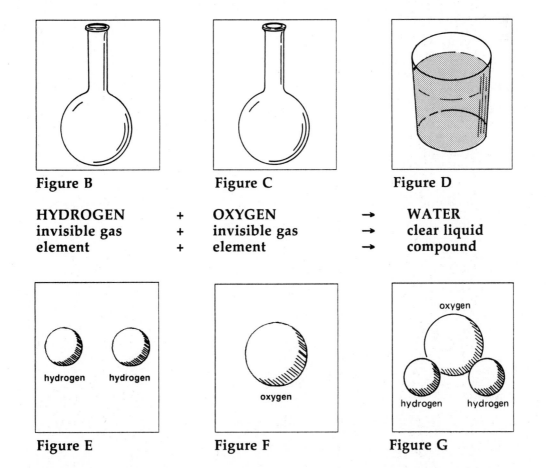

Figure B	**Figure C**	**Figure D**

HYDROGEN	**+**	**OXYGEN**	→	**WATER**
invisible gas	**+**	**invisible gas**	→	**clear liquid**
element	**+**	**element**	→	**compound**

Figure E	**Figure F**	**Figure G**

SALT

Table salt is a compound. It is made up of the elements sodium and chlorine.

Sodium is a dangerous metal. Chlorine is a poisonous gas.

They can link up to form a compound that our bodies need.

The compound is sodium chloride. We call it <u>salt</u>.

Figure H

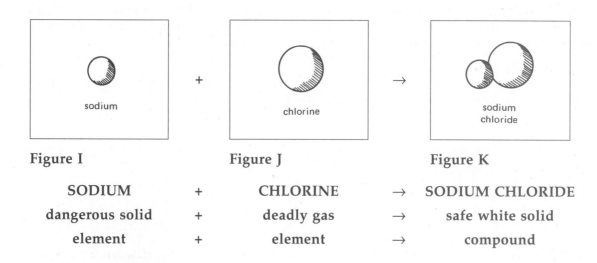

Figure I   **Figure J**   **Figure K**

SODIUM	+	CHLORINE	→	SODIUM CHLORIDE
dangerous solid	+	deadly gas	→	safe white solid
element	+	element	→	compound

CARBON DIOXIDE

<u>Carbon</u> <u>dioxide</u> is a gas compound. It is made of the elements carbon and oxygen.

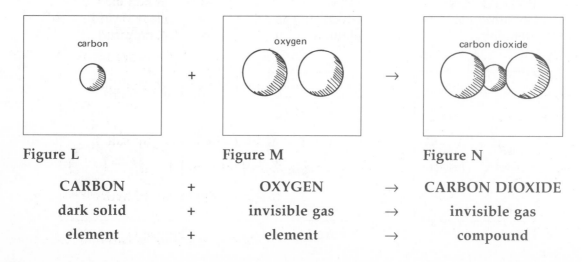

Figure L   **Figure M**   **Figure N**

CARBON	+	OXYGEN	→	CARBON DIOXIDE
dark solid	+	invisible gas	→	invisible gas
element	+	element	→	compound

FILL IN THE BLANK

Complete each statement using a term or terms from the list below. Write your answers in the spaces provided. Some words may be used more than once.

one million	millions	metal	molecule
compounds	109	elements	linked-up
nonmetal	lose	two	

1. There are _____ known metals.

2. The number of different known substances is more than _____

3. Elements combine to form _____ .

4. Elements of a compound _____ their properties.

5. A compound has a least _____ elements.

6. A compound must have at least one _____ atom and one

   _____ atom.

7. The smallest part of a compound is called a _____ .

8. In a small amount of a compound there may be _____ of molecules.

9. A compound is made of _____ atoms.

10. All matter is made up of _____ or _____ .

MATCHING

Match each term in Column A with its description in Column B. Write the correct letter in the space provided.

Column A	Column B
_____ 1. atom	a) has one kind of atom
_____ 2. molecule	b) short way of writing an element
_____ 3. symbol	c) smallest part of an element
_____ 4. element	d) two or more elements are linked together
_____ 5. compound	e) smallest part of a compound
_____ 6. water	f) salt
_____ 7. carbon dioxide	g) elements that make up salt
_____ 8. sodium and chlorine	h) links with a nonmetal
_____ 9. metal	i) compound made up of hydrogen and oxygen
_____ 10. sodium chloride	j) compound made up of carbon and oxygen

TRUE OR FALSE

In the space provided, write "true" if the sentence is true. Write "false" if the sentence is false.

_____   **1.** All matter is made of atoms.

_____   **2.** An element is matter.

_____   **3.** A compound is matter.

_____   **4.** All matter is made of elements or compounds.

_____   **5.** Elements and compounds are made of atoms.

_____   **6.** Compounds link up to make elements.

_____   **7.** A compound can have only one element.

_____   **8.** The smallest part of a compound is one atom of that compound.

_____   **9.** A compound must have at lest one metal atom and one nonmetal atom.

_____   **10.** There are more elements than compounds.

REACHING OUT

Why should you always follow instructions carefully when mixing chemicals.

_____

_____

_____

_____

_____

_____

What is a chemical formula?

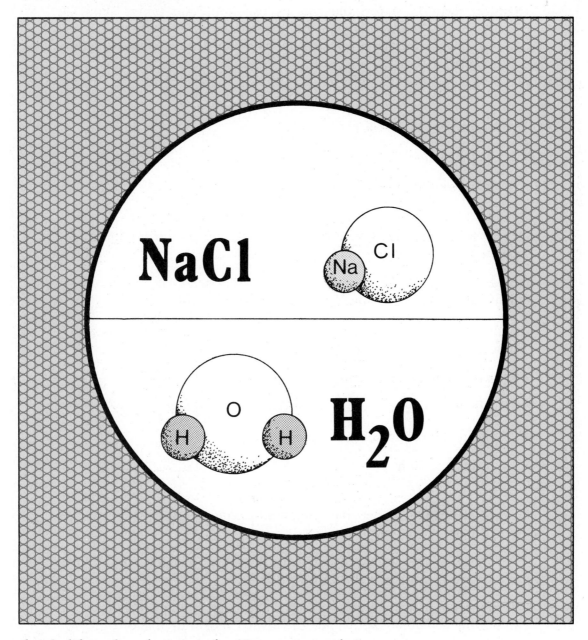

chemical formula: short way of writing a compound

LESSON 9 | What is a chemical formula?

Each element has its own chemical symbol. Each compound has its own **chemical formula**. A formula tells us two important things about a compound. It tells us what elements the compound is made of. It also tells us how many atoms of each element are in a molecule of the compound.

The formula for table salt is NaCl.

- Na is the symbol for sodium.

- Cl is the symbol for chlorine.

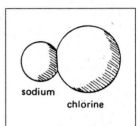

One molecule of NaCl has a total of two atoms. One of the atoms is sodium (Na). The other atom is chlorine (Cl).

Sometimes a symbol has a small number written next to it. This number tells us the number of atoms there are of that element.

The formula for water is H_2O.

- H is the symbol for hydrogen.

- O is the symbol for oxygen.

- H_2 means two atoms of hydrogen.

- O means one atom of oxygen.

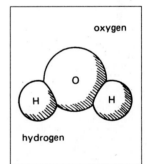

One molecule of H_2O, then, has a total of three atoms. Two of the atoms are hydrogen. One atom is oxygen.

The formula for a compound is always the same. A change in the formula means that a new substance was formed.

It is helpful to learn to recognize some chemical symbols. However, if you see one you do not know, you can always look it up in a dictionary, an encyclopedia, or a chemistry book.

SOME COMMON MOLECULES

Formula: HgO

Name: mercuric oxide

Elements: mercury (Hg) and oxygen (O)

Number of atoms in each element:
    1 atom of mercury (Hg)
    1 atom of oxygen (O)

Total number of atoms in one molecule:
    2 atoms total

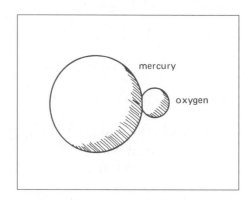

Figure A

Formula: KCl

Name: potassium chloride

Elements: potassium (K) and chlorine (Cl)

Number of atoms in each element:
    1 atom of potassium (K)
    1 atom of Chlorine (Cl)

Total number of atoms in one molecule:
    2 atoms total

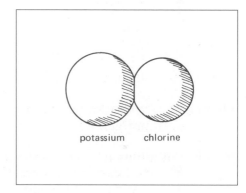

Figure B

Formula: NaOH

Name: sodium hydroxide (lye)

Elements: sodium (S), oxygen (O), and hydrogen (H)

Number of atoms in each element:
    1 atom of sodium (S)
    1 atom of oxygen (O)
    1 atom of hydrogen (H)

Total number of atoms in one molecule:
    3 atoms total

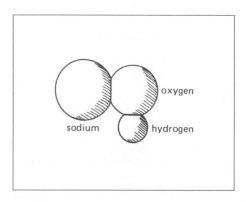

Figure C

MORE COMMON MOLECULES

Formula: Fe_2O_3

Name: iron oxide (rust)

Elements: iron (Fe) and oxygen (O)

Number of atoms in each element:
   2 atoms of iron (Fe)
   3 atoms o f oxygen (O)

Total number of atoms in one molecule:
   5 atoms total

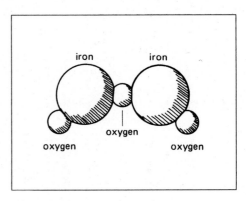

Figure D

Formula: H_2SO_4

Name: sulfuric acid

Elements: hydrogen (H), sulfur (S), and
   oxygen (O)

Number of atoms in each element:
   2 atoms of hydrogen (H)
   1 atom of sulfur (S)
   4 atoms of oxygen (O)

Total number of atoms in one molecule:
   7 atoms total

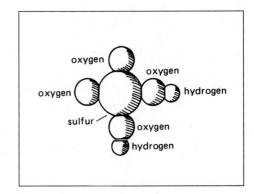

Figure E

Formula: $NaHCO_3$

Name: sodium hydrogen carbonate
   (baking soda)

Elements: sodium (Na), hydrogen (H),
   carbon (C), and oxygen (O)

Number of atoms in each element:
   1 atom of sodium (Na)
   1 atom of hydrogen (H)
   1 atom of carbon(C)
   3 atoms of oxygen (O)

Total number of atoms in one molecule:
   6 atoms total

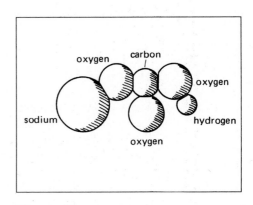

Figure F

COMPLETING SENTENCES

Choose the correct word or term for each statement. Write your choice in the spaces provided.

1. A molecule is made up of _____.

atoms, oxygen

2. A single molecule has at least _____ atoms.

one, two

3. _____ are combined to make _____.

Elements, Compounds   elements, compounds

4. There are _____ elements than compounds.

more, fewer

5. Molecules are usually _____ than atoms.

larger, smaller

The formula for starch is $C_6H_{10}O_5$. This stands for one molecule of starch. Answer these questions about the starch molecule.

6. Starch is made up of _____ elements.

one, two, three

7. The number of different <u>kinds</u> of atoms in starch is _____.

three, billions

8. One molecule of starch has _____ atoms of hydrogen.

two, six, ten

9. The total number of atoms in one molecule of starch is _____.

6, 10, 16, 21

10. The number of molecules in a teaspoon of starch is _____.

about one hundred, more than a billion

MATCHING

Match each term in Column A with its description in Column B. Write the correct letter in the space provided.

Column A	Column B
_____ 1. CaF_2	a) contains one kind of atom
_____ 2. HF	b) 3 atoms in each molecule
_____ 3. formula	c) 2 atoms in each molecule
_____ 4. element	d) short way of writing an element
_____ 5. symbol	e) short way of writing a compound

COMPLETE THE CHART

Complete the chart by filling in the missing information. The first one has been done for you.

Formula	Name	Number of Elements	Names of the Elements	Number of Atoms of Each Element	Total Number of Atoms In One Molecule
1. MgO	magnesium oxide	2	magnesium oxygen	1 1	2
2. SO_2	sulfur dioxide				
3. NH_3	ammonia				
4. H_2CO_3	carbonic acid (soda water)				
5. $C_{12}H_{22}O_{11}$	table sugar				
6. $MgSO_4$	Epsom salts				
7. NaOH	sodium hydroxide (lye)				
8. H_2O_2	hydrogen peroxide				
9. Fe_2O_3	iron oxide (rust)				
10. $NaHCO_3$	sodium bicarbonate (baking soda)				

How do elements form compounds?

borrow: to use something that belongs to someone or something else
inert gases: elements which have complete outer electron shells, gases which rarely react with other elements.
lend: to let someone use something that belongs to you
noble gases: inert gases
shells: energy levels in which electrons are arranged around the nucleus
stable: is not likely to change, prefers to stay the way it is

LESSON 10 | How do elements form compounds?

You know that the electrons in atoms orbit the nucleus. You also know that electrons are arranged in shells around the atom.

What you probably did not know (but soon will) is that atoms "want" to have two, eight, or eighteen electrons in their outer shells. Atoms with two, eight, or eighteen electrons in their outer shells are more **stable** than atoms with some other number of electrons in their outer shell.

In order to have a stable outer electron shell, atoms link up and share electrons. Atoms that link up form molecules. This is how elements combine to form compounds.

When two atoms link up, one atom **borrows** electrons <u>from</u> another atom. The second atom **lends** its electrons <u>to</u> the first atom.

<u>Metals</u> usually have <u>less</u> than four electrons in their outer shell. <u>Non-metals</u> usually have <u>more</u> than four electrons in their outer shell. <u>Metals lend</u> electrons to nonmetals. <u>Nonmetals borrow</u> electrons from metals.

For example, sodium has one electron in its outer shell (M shell). Chlorine has seven electrons in its outer shell (M shell). Sodium and chlorine can combine to form sodium chloride. The sodium atom lends the only electron in its M shell to the chlorine atom. Sodium now has eight electrons in its outer shell (now the L shell), and chlorine has eight electrons in its outer shell (still the M shell).

Some atoms which already have very stable outer shells do not link up with any other elements. Also, just because an atom <u>can</u> combine with another atom does <u>not</u> mean that it <u>will</u> combine with the other atom.

Sodium and chlorine combine to form sodium chloride.

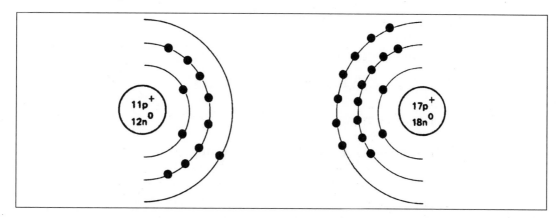

Figure A *Sodium has one electron in its outer shell (M shell) and chlorine has seven electrons in its outer shell (M shell).*

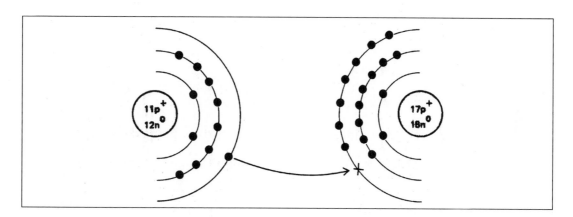

Figure B *The sodium atom lends the only electron in its M shell to the chlorine atom.*

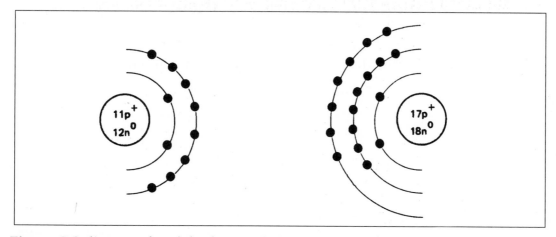

Figure C *Sodium now has eight electrons in its outer shell (now the L shell), and chlorine has eight electrons in its outer shell (still the M shell).*

Now answer the following questions.

1. How many outer-ring electrons does sodium have?_____

2. Is sodium's outer shell stable? _____

3. Is sodium a metal or a nonmetal? _____

4. How many outer-ring electrons does chlorine have?_____

5. Is chlorine's outer shell stable? _____

6. Is chlorine a metal or a nonmetal?_____

7. Altogether, how many outer-ring electrons do sodium and chlorine have? (Count them.) _____

8. Together, can they make a stable shell? _____

9. Which atom is the electron "lender"? _____

10. How many electrons are lent? _____

11. Which atom borrows the electron?_____

12. How many electrons are borrowed? _____

13. Do they make a compound? _____

14. When sodium and chlorine link up, do their properties change? _____

15. What is the name of the compound sodium and chlorine make? _____

COMPLETING SENTENCES

Choose the correct word or term for each statement. Write your choice in the spaces provided.

1. The outer ring of a metal has _____ than four electrons.
   <u>fewer, more</u>

2. Metals _____ electrons.
   <u>lend, borrow</u>

3. The outer ring of a nonmetal has _____ than four electrons.
   <u>fewer, more</u>

4. Nonmetals _____ electrons.
   <u>lend, borrow</u>

5. Most elements are_____ .
   <u>metals, nonmetals</u>

Calcium and oxygen join to form the compound calcium oxide (CaO).

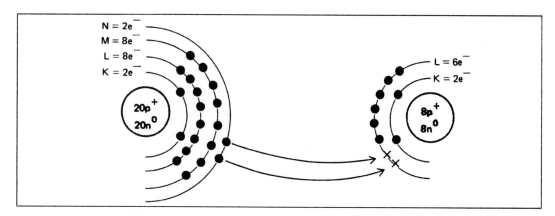

Figure D

Answer the following questions.

1. How many outer-ring electrons does calcium have? _____

2. Is this a stable shell? _____

3. Is calcium a metal or nonmetal? _____

4. How many outer-ring electrons does oxygen have? _____

5. Is this a stable shell? _____

6. Is oxygen a metal or a nonmetal? _____

7. Altogether, how many outer-ring electrons do calcium and oxygen have? (Count

    them.) _____

8. Together, can they make a stable shell? _____

9. Which atom lends electrons? _____

10. How many electrons are lent? _____

11. Which atom borrows the electrons? _____

12. How many electrons are borrowed? _____

13. Do they form a compound? _____

14. When calcium and oxygen link up, do their properties change? _____

15. What is the name of the compound oxygen and calcium form? _____

COMPLETE THE CHART

Complete the chart by filling in the missing information. The first has been done for you.

Element	Number of Electrons in Outer Ring	Metal or Nonmetal?	Electron Lender or Borrower?	Lends or Borrows How Many Electrons?
1. calcium	2	metal	lender	2
2. copper				
3. phosphorus				
4. potassium				
5. oxygen				
6. iodine				
7. gold				
8. bromine				
9. sulfur				
10. cobalt				

TRUE OR FALSE

In the space provided, write "true" if the sentence is true. Write "false" if the sentence is false.

_____ 1. Atoms with fewer than 4 outer electrons lend electrons.

_____ 2. Atoms with more than 4 outer electrons borrow electrons.

_____ 3. Metals lend electrons.

_____ 4. Nonmetals lend electrons.

_____ 5. Atoms lend and borrow electrons from inner shells.

_____ 6. Only outer shells gain or lose electrons with other atoms.

_____ 7. All atoms form compounds.

_____ 8. Every element can link up with every other element.

_____ 9. Atoms with more than 4 outer electrons are metals.

_____ 10. Atoms with more than 4 outer electrons are nonmetals.

COMPLETE THE CHART

Complete the chart by filling in the missing information. The first has been done for you.

The elements in Group 18 do not lend or borrow electrons because their outer electron shell is naturally stable. They are often called **noble gases** or **inert gases** because they do not combine with other elements.

Elements of Group	Lend Electrons?	Borrow Electrons?	Metal or Nonmetal?
1	Yes	No	metal
2			
3			
4			
5			
6			
8			
15			
16			
17			
18			

MATCHING

Match each term in Column A with its description in Column B. Write the correct letter in the space provided.

Column A

_____ 1. metals

_____ 2. two, eight, and eighteen

_____ 3. sodium and chlorine

_____ 4. hydrogen and oxygen

_____ 5. nonmetals

Column B

a) link up to form water

b) link up to form salt

c) number of electrons in a stable outer ring

d) borrow electrons

e) lend electrons

Calcium and chlorine link up to form calcium chloride. Look at the diagrams of these atoms. Fill in the missing parts on each diagram. Then answer the questions.

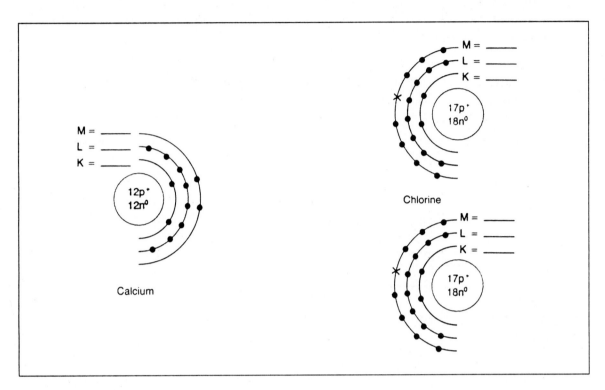

Figure E

1. How many outer-ring electrons does a calcium atom have?_____

2. How many outer-ring electrons does a chlorine atom have?_____

3. Which atom lends electrons? _____

4. How many electrons does <u>one</u> atom of this element lend? _____

5. Which atom borrows electrons? _____

6. How many electrons does <u>one</u> atom of this element borrow? _____

7. How many chlorine atoms are needed to link up with *one* calcium atom? Explain.

   _____

   _____

   _____

8. What is the formula for calcium chloride? _____

What is the difference between a physical change and a chemical change?

11

chemical change: change in matter that produces new substances
chemical reaction: process involving a chemical change
physical change: a change in matter that does not produce any new products or substances

LESSON 11

What is the difference between a physical change and a chemical change?

There are different ways you can change things. For example, you can tear up a piece of paper into small pieces. What remains is still paper. You have changed the way the paper looks. But you have not made any new substance. You have made a physical change.

If, instead, you burned the paper, what would be left? What is left is no longer paper. In this case the substance has been changed. This is a chemical change.

A **physical change** does not change the way the atoms are linked up. The substance may look different, but no new substance has been formed. The chemical properties are not changed.

In a physical change, no energy is taken in or given off <u>unless</u> there is a change of state.

In a **chemical change**, matter changes from one kind of material to another kind of material. The atoms that make up the material <u>do not</u> change. Instead, the atoms change the way they are linked up. The new substances can have very different properties than the old substances.

Chemical changes take place during chemical reactions. In a **chemical reaction** there is never a change in the number of elements. There is never a change in the number of atoms of an one element. No elements are lost. No new elements are added. They just combine in different ways.

Energy is always part of a chemical reaction. In a chemical reaction, energy is either taken in or given off.

Electrolysis is an example of a <u>chemical change</u>. Electrical energy is used to break water molecules apart into oxygen and hydrogen. Figure B shows a diagram of the chemical reaction taking place during electrolysis. The molecules on the <u>left</u> side of the arrow were present before the electrolysis took place. The molecules on the <u>right</u> side of the arrow were present <u>after</u> the electrolysis took place. Look at the diagram and then answer the questions below.

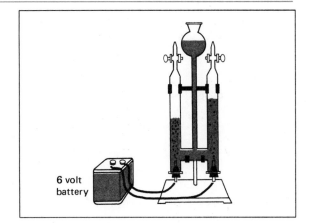

Figure A

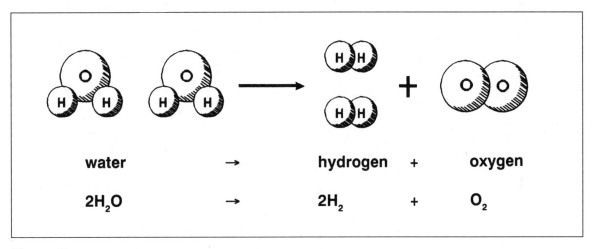

Figure B

1. What compound did we start with? _____

2. What two elements make up that compound?_____ _____

3. What two elements did we end up with?_____ _____

4. Were new substances formed? _____

5. Are the properties of the old and new substance different?_____

6. How many atoms of hydrogen did we start with? _____

7. How many atoms of oxygen did we start with? _____

8. How many atoms of hydrogen did we end up with?_____

9. How many atoms of oxygen did we end up with?_____

10. Did the type and number of atoms change? _____

11. Does electrolysis cause a chemical change or physical change? _____

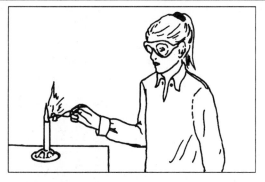

Figure C

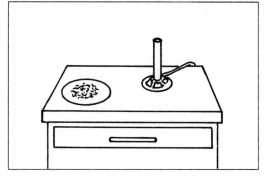

Figure D

Burning magnesium is another example of a <u>chemical change</u>. When magnesium is burned, the magnesium combines with oxygen in the air to form magnesium oxide. Study Figure E and then answer the questions below.

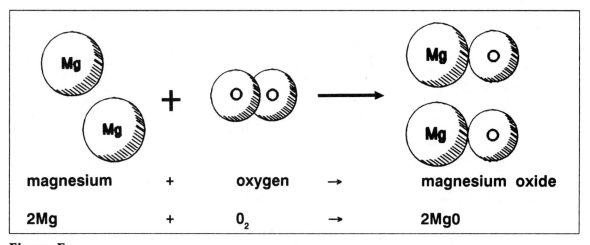

Figure E

1. What two elements did we start with? _____ _____

2. What compound did we end up with? _____

3. What two elements make up that compound? _____ _____

4. Were new substances formed? _____

5. Are the properties of the old and new substance different? _____

6. How many atoms of magnesium did we start with? _____

7. How many atoms of oxygen did we start with? _____

8. How many atoms of magnesium did we end up with? _____

9. How many atoms of oxygen did we end up with? _____

10. Did the type and number of atoms change? _____

11. Does burning magnesium cause a chemical change or physical change? _____

Shredding paper is an example of a physical change. In a physical change, the atoms do not change the way they linked up. No new products are formed. Look at Figure F and then answer the questions below.

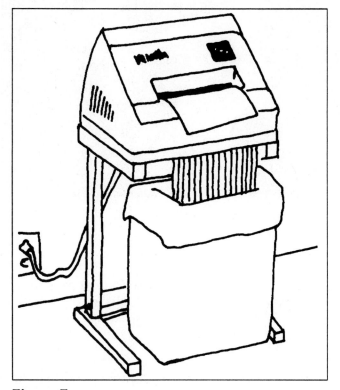

Figure F

1. Does the paper look different after being shredded? ——————————

2. Is the paper still paper? _____

3. Are the atoms taking in energy?_____

4. Are the atoms giving off energy? _____

5. In a physical change, the atoms_____ change the way they link up.
   do, do not

6. The chemical properties of the paper _____ changed.
   do, do not

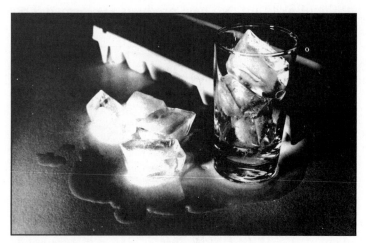

Figure G

Melting ice is an example of a change of state. A solid (ice) changes into a liquid (water). The formula for water is H$_2$O. The formula for ice <u>also</u> is H$_2$O. Both ice and water have the same chemical formula. Therefore no chemical change takes place. A change of state (such as melting ice) is a <u>physical change</u>.

Energy is taken in when ice is melted. Changes of state are the only physical changes where energy is taken in or given off. Look at Figure G and then answer the questions below.

1. Does the ice look different after it is melted?_____

2. When ice changes to water, the link-up of the atoms _____ change.
does, does not

3. When water changes to ice, the link-up of the atoms_____ change.
does, does not

4. The melting of ice is an example of a _____ change.
physical, chemical

5. When ice changes to a liquid, the ice _____ take in energy.
does, does not

6. Usually, energy _____ part of a physical change.
is, is not

7. Energy is part of a physical change only when there is _____.
electrolysis, a change of state

Figure H

Look at Figure H and then answer the questions below.

1. Does the wood look different after being chopped? _____

2. Is the wood still wood? _____

3. Are the atoms changing the way they are linked up? _____

4. Are any elements being added? _____

5. Are any elements being lost? _____

6. Are any new products being formed? _____

7. Is the wood taking in energy? _____

8. Is the wood giving off energy? _____

9. The chopping of wood is an example of a _____ change.

physical, chemical

10. What is the difference between a physical change and a chemical change?

    _____

    _____

TRUE OR FALSE

In the space provided, write "true" if the sentence is true. Write "false" if the sentence is false.

_____ 1. A chemical reaction causes a chemical change.

_____ 2. A chemical change makes new products.

_____ 3. Elements can be lost or gained in a chemical reaction.

_____ 4. Energy can be taken in only during a chemical reaction.

_____ 5. The substances that take part in a chemical reaction keep their properties.

_____ 6. The new substances made in a chemical reaction have new properties.

_____ 7. A physical change makes new products.

_____ 8. The boiling of water is an example of a chemical change.

_____ 9. The electrolysis of water is an example of a chemical change.

_____ 10. Some physical changes involve taking in or giving off energy.

CHEMICAL CHANGE OR PHYSICAL CHANGE?

Tell whether each of the following is a chemical change or a physical change.

1. mixing salt and pepper _____

2. evaporation of water _____

3. electrolysis of water _____

4. cutting a marshmallow _____

5. toasting a marshmallow _____

6. burning magnesium _____

7. demolishing a car _____

8. the rusting of iron _____

9. melting of sugar _____

10. baking a cake _____

How is a mixture different from a compound?

12

mixture: two or more substances that are physically combined

LESSON 12 | How is a mixture different from a compound?

Sometimes two or more substances are mixed together. They do not combine chemically. They do not make a compound. They make a **mixture**. The substances are <u>physically</u> combined. None of the substances in the mixture has been changed chemically. No chemical reaction has take place. No new substances are formed.

Vegetable soup is an example of a mixture. So is salt and sand mixed together. You can still tell one part from the other.

What are the difference between a compound and a mixture? The chart below lists some of the differences.

MIXTURE	COMPOUND
The parts of a mixture do not change their properties.	The elements that make up a compound lose their chemical properties. The new compound has its own chemical properties.
The ratio between the parts of a mixture may be any amount.	The ratio between the parts of a mixture is a fixed amount.
Energy is not taken in or given off when a mixture is made or separated.	Energy is always taken in or given off when a compound is broken up or put together.
A mixture can be separated by physical means. For example, a strainer can separate some mixtures.	A compound can be separated only by with a chemical reaction. For example, electrolysis changes water (H_2O) into hydrogen and oxygen.

ABOUT MIXTURES

A mixture can have many kinds of matter. It can have:

elements only   or   compounds only   or elements and compounds

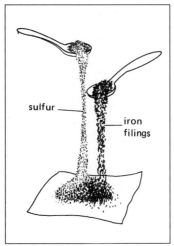

Figure A

Figure B

Figure C

SALT AND PEPPER

Salt mixed with pepper is an example of a mixture. The salt and pepper are just close together. They do not react together. Properties do not change. The salt is still salt. The pepper is still pepper. No new products are formed.

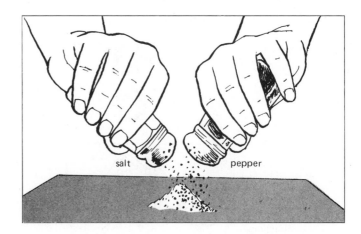

It makes no difference how much pepper or salt there is. No exact amounts are needed. Energy is not taken in or given off by the molecules of the salt or the pepper.

Salt is a compound. Pepper is a compound. Salt with pepper is a mixture made up of two compounds.

TRUE OR FALSE

In the space provided, write "true" if the sentence is true. Write "false" if the sentence is false.

_____ 1. A ratio of the parts of a mixture are exact.

_____ 2. A ratio of the parts of a compound are exact.

_____ 3. The parts of a mixture keep their properties.

_____ 4. The elements of a compound keep their properties.

_____ 5. We need energy to make or break up a compound.

_____ 6. Hydrogen is a compound.

_____ 7. Water is a compound.

_____ 8. We need a chemical reaction to separate a compound.

_____ 9. Electricity can separate some compounds.

_____ 10. A magnet can separate water into oxygen and hydrogen.

MAKING A MIXTURE AND A COMPOUND

PART I   Making a Mixture

What You Need (Materials)

iron filings
powdered yellow sulfur
magnet
piece of paper
teaspoon

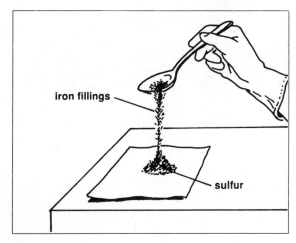

Figure E   **Figure F**

How To Do the Experiment (Procedure)

1. Place a teaspoon of the sulfur on a piece of paper (Figure E).

2. Add about 2/3 teaspoon of iron filings.

3. Mix them together.

4. Hold the magnet in the mixture. Move it around (Figure F).

5. Lift the magnet.

What You Learned (Observations)

1. Could you tell the sulfur from the iron before using the magnet?_____

2. The magnet lifted the _____.

sulfur, iron

3. The magnet did not lift the _____.

iron, sulfur

4. Have you separated the iron from the sulfur? _____

Something To Think About (Conclusions)

1. Did the properties of the iron change? _____

2. Did the properties of the sulfur change?_____

3. Was a new product formed? _____

4. Did a chemical reaction take place? _____

5. Iron filings and sulfur together make a _____ .

6. There _____ a chemical change.

was, was not

PART II   Making a Compound

What You Need (Materials)

iron filings   magnet
powdered yellow sulfur   piece of paper
test tube and holder   teaspoon
Bunsen burner   hammer
ringstand and clamp   cloth

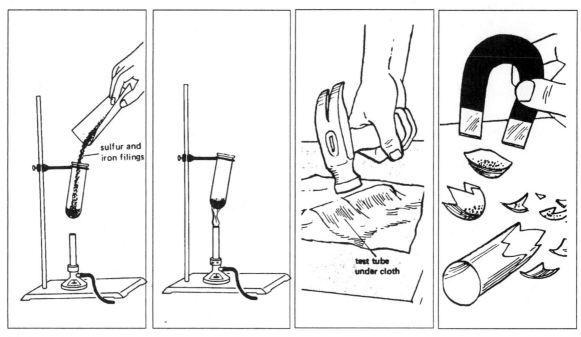

Figure G   Figure H   Figure I   Figure J

How To Do The Experiment (Procedure)

1. Remove the iron filings from the magnet. Mix them in with the sulfur.

2. Pour the iron filings into the test tube (Figure G).

3. Heat the test tube over the Bunsen burner until the sulfur melts (Figure H).

4. Remove the test tube from the flame. Let the tube cool.

5. Cover the tube with a cloth. Then break it by carefully tapping the bottom of the test tube with a hammer (Figure I).

6. Remove the cloth. Examine the substance that was in the test tube.

7. Put the magnet on the substance (Figure J).

8. Lift the magnet.

1. Could you tell the sulfur from the iron after they were heated together? _____

2. Did the magnet lift the iron filings? _____

3. Did the properties of the iron change? _____

4. Did the properties of the sulfur change? _____

Something To Think About (Conclusions)

1. Was a new product formed? _____

2. Did a chemical reaction take place? _____

3. Sulfur and iron filings heated together make a _____ .

   mixture, compound

4. The formula for the compound made when the iron and sulfur were heated is FeS.

   Take a guess—the compound made from iron and sulfur is called _____ .

   iron oxide, iron sulfide

MIXTURE OR COMPOUND

The chart below lists some terms and phrases that describe mixtures and compounds. Which ones describe mixtures? Which describe compounds? Put a check [✓] in the space to show your choice.

		Mixture	Compound
1.	properties change		
2.	properties do not change		
3.	exact ratios of elements		
4.	no exact ratios of elements		
5.	energy always taken in or given off		
6.	energy not taken in or given off		
7.	separated by chemical means		
8.	separated by physical means		
9.	a pile of iron filings and sulfur		
10.	iron sulfide		

SCIENCE *EXTRA*

Buckyballs

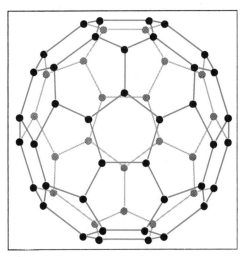 

Atoms can form molecules in a number of ways. Scientists are always trying to discover new ways that atoms bond together. In 1985, Richard Smalley and Harold Kroto were seeing what types of molecules would form when they heated carbon atoms to 8,000°C (14,500°F). They discovered something remarkable — a new form of carbon.

Before this discovery, scientists knew of only two types of molecules that carbon atoms could form, graphite and diamonds. Graphite is made up of layers of carbon atoms. Graphite is found in pencils and is often incorrectly called "pencil lead." Diamonds are also made up of pure carbon. The carbon atoms in diamonds are arranged in an octohedral (eight sided) form. This structure makes diamonds very strong.

Naturally, Smalley and Kroto were very excited when they discovered a third form of carbon. What was the shape of this new molecule? The chemists ran some tests and discovered two things—the new molecule has sixty atoms and the molecule had no "edges." An "edge" is a place on a molecule for other atoms or molecules to link onto easily.

The shape that fit this description was a sphere, or more exactly, a geodesic [jee-uh-DES-ik] dome. In honor of Buckminster Fuller, the inventor of the geodesic dome, the new molecules are called buckyballs.

Because buckyballs are round, they spin very, very fast — up to a billion times a second! This makes it impossible to use powerful microcopes to take pictures of buckyballs. Without a picture of a buckyball, no one could prove that they were really shaped like a geodesic dome.

That was until Joel Hawkins and a group of chemists from the University of California at Berkeley developed a method of "grabbing" a buckyball by attaching it to another molecule. This stopped the buckyball from spinning so that a picture could be taken.

Now that the existence of buckyballs has been confirmed, scientists are working even harder to discover ways to make use of it. After all, it's not every day that a new form of carbon is discovered.

How can mixtures be separated?

dissolve: to make a solid matter disappear in a liquid
evaporate [i-VAP-uh-rayt]: change from a liquid to a gas

LESSON 13 | How can mixtures be separated?

When you separate a mixture, you just separate the parts. You do not separate the linked-up atoms. Mixtures are separated without any chemical reaction.

There are many different kinds of mixtures. Different mixtures are separated in different ways. There are four main ways to separate a mixture. They are:

STRAINING Straining separates matter by size. A strainer has holes. Any matter that is smaller than the holes passes through the holes. Anything larger than the holes stays in the strainer. Strainers come in different sizes—some have large holes, some have small holes.

Filter paper is a kind of strainer. Filter paper has very tiny holes. It separates tiny pieces of solids from the liquids they are mixed with.

USING A MAGNET A magnet separates iron parts form a mixture.

EVAPORATION When some substances mix with water, they seem to disappear. Think of sugar and water. In water, sugar seems to disappear. The sugar **dissolves**. Solids can dissolved in other liquids, as well. However, not all solids can be dissolved. Think of sand in water. Does sand dissolve in water?

Sugar and water are a mixture, <u>not </u>a compound. The sugar molecules do <u>not </u>change. You can taste the sugar even thought you cannot see it. If you let the water evaporate, the sugar will remain. The sugar will <u>not</u> evaporate. Mixtures like sugar and water can be separated using evaporation. a liquid will **evaporate** [i-VAP-uh-rayt] faster if you heat it.

DISSOLVING Dissolving is sometimes helpful when you want to separate a mixture. Think of a mixture of sugar and sand. If you put this mixture in water, the sugar will dissolve. The sand will not dissolve. Now you can filter out the sand from the water. Then, you can evaporate the water leaving the sugar behind.

WHAT DO THE PICTURES SHOW?

Five of the pictures below show a mixture being separated. The other picture shows a step needed before separation can be done.

Look at each picture. Then answer the question on the next page. Write the letter of the right picture for each question.

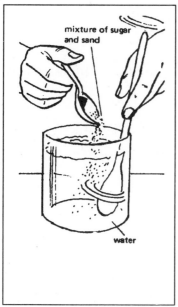

Figure A

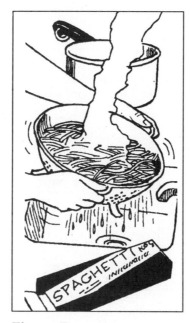

Figure B

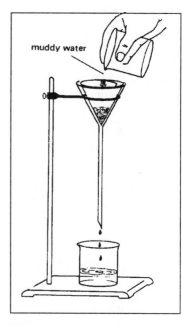

Figure C

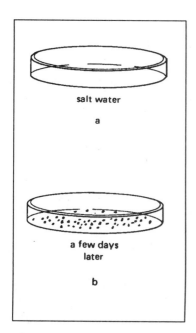

Figure D

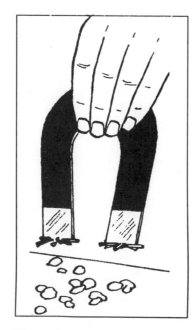

Figure E

Figure F

1. Which pictures show straining? _____ _____

2. Which picture shows filter paper being used? _____

3. Which picture shows pieces of iron being separated? _____

4. Which picture shows dissolving? _____

5. Which picture shows evaporation? _____

FILL IN THE BLANK

Complete each statement using a term or terms from the list below. Write your answers in the spaces provided. Some words may be used more than once.

mixture	straining	iron
air	size	using a magnet
dissolving	dissolve	strainer
evaporation	filter paper	holes
heated		

1. Four ways to separate mixtures are: _____ , _____ ,

   _____ and _____ .

2. Straining separates matter according to _____ .

3. A _____ separates matter by size.

4. A strainer has many _____ .

5. We can separate a mixture of very tiny solid pieces and water by using

   _____ .

6. We use a magnet to separate _____ from a mixture.

7. When water evaporates, the vapor escapes in the _____ .

8. A solid that seems to disappear in a liquid is said to _____ .

9. Sugar and water are a _____ .

10. A liquid will evaporate faster if it is _____ .

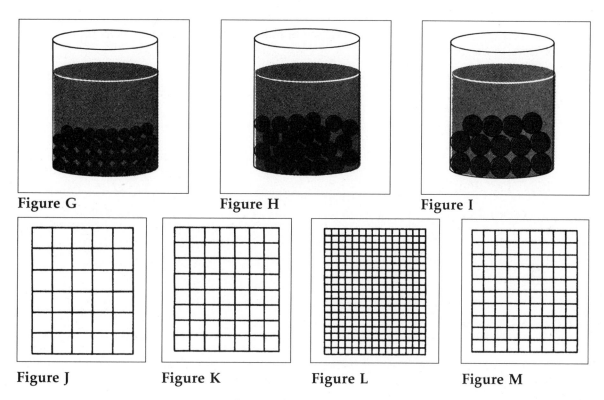

Figure G   Figure H   Figure I

Figure J   Figure K   Figure L   Figure M

Figures G, H, and I each show a glass of water with marbles in it. Figures J, K, L, and M each show a screen strainer. Using a metric ruler, measure the marbles in each glass. Then measure the size of one of the openings in each strainer. Complete each of the statements below using the term or terms form the list below.

strainer J	strainer L	3 mm	4 mm	5 mm
strainer K	2 mm	3.5 mm	4.5 mm	6 mm

1. The marbles in Figure G measure _____ across.

2. The marbles in Figure H measure _____ across.

3. The marbles in Figure I measure _____ across.

4. The openings in Figure J measure _____ across.

5. The openings in Figure K measure _____ across.

6. The openings in Figure L measure _____ across.

7. The openings in Figure M measure _____ across.

8. _____ will separate all the shown solids from the water

9. _____ will separate none of the shown solids from the water.

10. _____ is the largest strainer that can separate the solids in glass H.

WORD SCRAMBLE

Below are several scrambled words you have used in this Lesson. Unscramble the words and write your answers in the spaces provided.

1. VISOLEDS   _____

2. AVOPEATER   _____

3. TIREXUM   _____

4. MONDOCUP   _____

5. TAGMEN   _____

TRUE OR FALSE

In the space provided, write "true" if the sentence is true. Write "false" if the sentence is false.

_____   **1.**   Straining causes a chemical change.

_____   **2.**   Evaporation causes a chemical change.

_____   **3.**   A magnet causes physical change.

_____   **4.**   Dissolving causes a physical change.

_____   **5.**   Filter paper has large holes.

_____   **6.**   Only scientists use strainers.

_____   **7.**   When a liquid evaporates, it goes into the air.

_____   **8.**   Sugar dissolved in water is still sugar.

_____   **9.**   A magnet can separate a mixture of paper clips and rubber bands.

_____   **10.**   Hot water evaporates faster than cold water.

HOW WOULD YOU SEPARATE THESE MIXTURES?

Five kinds of mixtures are listed below. Can you decide how to separate these mixtures? Before making up your mind, study the diagrams. Each diagram shows a different step used in separating mixtures.

Mixture 1   salt and iron filings
Mixture 2   salty water
Mixture 3   salt, iron filings, and water
Mixture 4   gravel, sand, and sugar
Mixture 5   gravel, sand, sugar, and iron filings

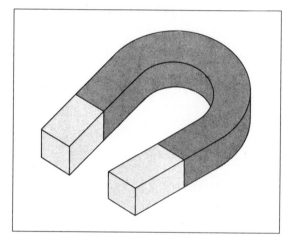

Figure N *A magnet is used to separate iron.*

Figure O *Water is used to dissolve a solid.*

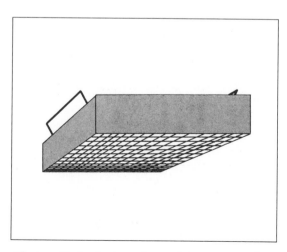

Figure P *A strainer is used to separate large solids.*

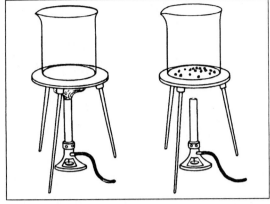

Figure Q *Evaporation is used to separate already dissolved solids.*

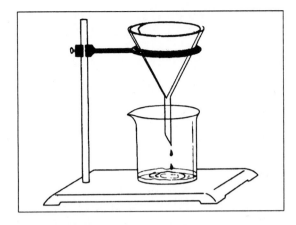

Figure R *Filtration is used to separate very small solids.*

Now decide which step or steps are needed to separate mixtures 1 through 5. In the blank spaces below, write down the steps you would use. In most cases, the order in which the steps are taken is not important.

Mixture 1: salt and iron filings (only one step is needed)

    Step 1: _____

Mixture 2: salt water (only one step is needed)

    Step 1: _____

Mixture 3: salt, iron filings, and water (two steps are needed)

    Step 1: _____

    Step 2: _____

Mixture 4: gravel, sand, and sugar (four steps are needed)

    Step 1: _____

    Step 2: _____

    Step 3: _____

    Step 4: _____

Mixture 5: gravel, sand sugar, and iron filings (five steps are needed)

    Step 1: _____

    Step 2: _____

    Step 3: _____

    Step 4: _____

    Step 5: _____

What is a suspension?

14

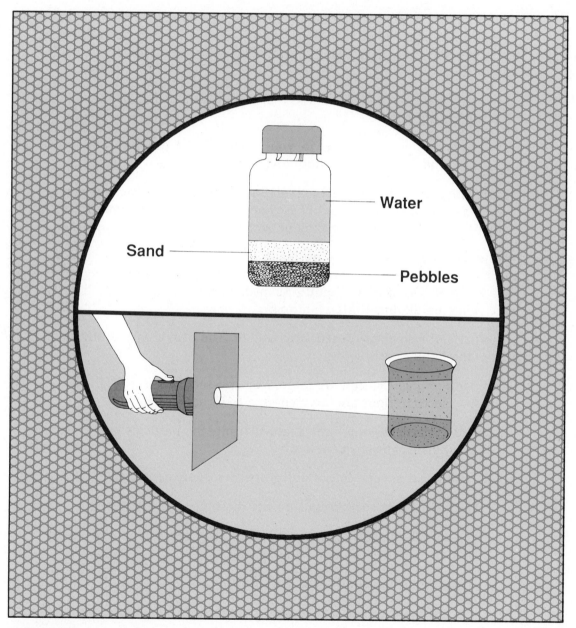

Water

Sand

Pebbles

colloids [KAHL-oydz]: suspension in which the particles are permanently suspended

emulsions [i-MUL-shunz]: suspension of two liquids

suspensions [suh-SPEN-shun]: cloudy mixture of two or more substances that settle on standing

Tyndall effect: scattering of a light beam by particles in a colloid

LESSON 14 | What is a suspension?

Before you pour orange juice, you shake it. Before you spoon out vegetable soup, you stir it.

Orange juice and vegetable soup are mixtures. But they are not like liquid solutions. The parts of liquid solutions dissolve and do not settle. Mixtures like orange juice and vegetable soup do not dissolve. The parts do settle out.

Mixtures that do <u>not</u> dissolve and that <u>do</u> settle are called **suspensions** [suh-SPEN-shunz].

You have many suspensions in your home. Salad dressing and fruit juices are suspensions. So is liquid shoe polish.

Have you ever read the label on a salad dressing bottle. Some labels may say "Shake well before using." These bottles contain suspensions. In fact, any mixture that you see settling or that needs mixing in a suspension.

Many common suspensions are made of solids and liquids. A suspension can be made of solids and gases, too. A suspension may even be made up of two or more liquids. Suspensions made up of only liquids are called **emulsions** [i-MUL-shunz].

The parts of a suspension settle by weight. The heavy parts settle first. Then the lighter parts settle.

The parts of a suspension are large. You can see them easily. Even the "small" pieces of flour are large enough to be seen easily.

Suspended particles stop light. Light that hits the particles is reflected. This is why suspensions are cloudy.

Now you know several important properties of suspensions:

- The particles in suspensions do not dissolve.

- The particles in suspensions settle out. They separate into layers by weight.

- Suspensions are cloudy and uneven.

- The solid particles of a suspension are large. You can see them.

- Suspended solids reflect light.

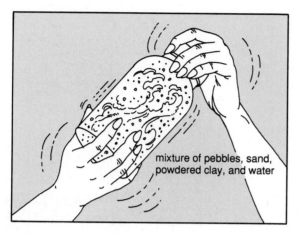

Figure A   **Figure B**

Place some pebbles, sand, and powdered clay into a jar.

Add water nearly to the top. Cover the jar tightly and shake.

Let it stand for five minutes. Observe what happens.

1. Which pieces settled first? _____

2. They are the _____ pieces.
    largest, smallest

3. They also are the _____ pieces.
    lighest, heaviest

4. Which settled last? _____

5. They are the _____ .
    largest, smallest

6. They also are the _____ .
    lightest, heaviest

7. This shows that when a suspension settles, the _____ pieces settle
    heaviest, lightest

    first and the _____ pieces settle last.
    heaviest, lightest

8. Usually, the heavy pieces are _____ ; the light pieces are
    smaller, larger

    _____ .
    smaller, larger

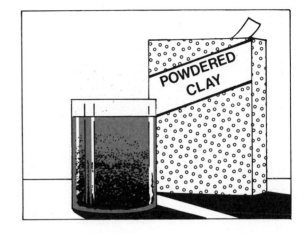

Figure C   **Figure D**

Stir some powdered clay into a jar of water. Let it stand. Notice what happens.

1. Powdered clay in water_____ a mixture.

is, is not

2. The clay_____ dissolve.

does, does not

3. The clay pieces _____ settle.

do, do not

4. Clay in water makes a mixture called a _____ .

liquid solution, suspension

5. The parts of a suspension _____ dissolve.

do, donot

6. The parts of a suspension _____ settle out.

do, do not

MATCHING

Match each term in Column A with its description in Column B. Write the correct letter in the space provided.

Column A	Column B
_____ **1.** mixture	**a)** reflect light
_____ **2.** suspension	**b)** settle last
_____ **3.** heavy pieces	**c)** cloudy mixture of two or more substances that settle on standing
_____ **4.** light pieces	**d)** liquid suspension
_____ **5.** emulsion	**e)** settle first

WHAT IS THE TYNDALL EFFECT?

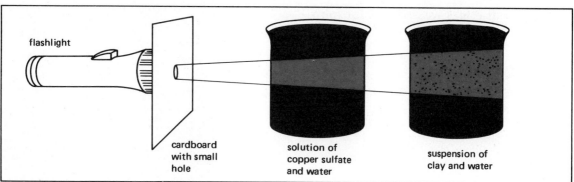

Figure E

What You Need (Materials)

2 beakers	powdered clay
copper sulfate	flashlight
water	cardboard with a hole

What to Do (Procedure)

1. Fill a beaker with a solution of copper sulfate and water.

2. Fill another beaker with a suspension of clay and water. Mix it well.

3. Place the beakers on the table next to one another.

4. Let the clay water settle for about two minutes.

5. Shine a flashlight through both beakers as in Figure B.

What You Saw and Learned (Observations)

1. You _____ see particles in the liquid solution.

can, cannot

2. You _____ see particles in the suspension.

can, cannot

The reflection of light by suspended particles is called the Tyndall effect.

3. You can see suspended particles because they _____ stop light.

do, do not

Something To Think About (Conclusions)

1. The Tyndall effect _____ help up identify a suspension.

does, does not

2. The Tyndall effect also helps us identify the _____ of suspended particles.

size, kind

3. Which kind of mixture shows the Tyndall effect? _____

solution, suspension

4. Which kind of mixture does not show the Tyndall effect? _____

solution, suspension

The Tyndall effect was named for John Tyndall. He was a 19th century British scientist.

He studied many things. One was how light passes through the air in different places.

Figure F

	Solutions	Suspensions
1. Do the parts dissolve?		
2. Do the particles settle?		
3. Is the mixture clear?		
4. Is the mixture cloudy?		
5. Do the particles reflect light?		
6. Can you see the particles?		

TRUE OR FALSE

In the space provided, write "true" if the sentence is true. Write "false" if the sentence is false.

_____ **1.** Suspensions are mixtures.

_____ **2.** The particles in suspensions settle out.

_____ **3.** Suspensions are transparent.

_____ **4.** Suspensions are cloudy.

_____ **5.** Suspended pieces settle by weight.

_____ **6.** In a suspension, heavy pieces settle last.

_____ **7.** Suspension particles ar the size of molecules.

_____ **8.** The particles in suspensions stop light.

COLLOIDS

You have learned that the solid parts of a regular suspension settle out. A **colloid** [KAHL-oyd] is a special kind of suspension. The solid particles in a colloid <u>do not</u> settle out.

The particles in a colloid are large than molecules. But they are much smaller than the particles in a regular suspension. The particles are so small and so light that they stay in suspension. They do not settle by themselves.

Most colloids look like liquid solutions—transparent and evenly mixed. You cannot see the suspended particles easily. But with the beam of light, the tiny particles show up in the Tyndall test. Some colloid particles are so small that you need a microscope to see them.

Colloids cannot be separated with filter paper. Special porcelain [POR-suh-lan] filters are needed.

COLLOID OR SOLUTION?

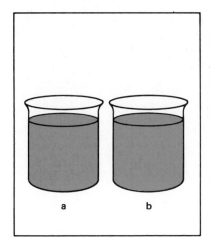 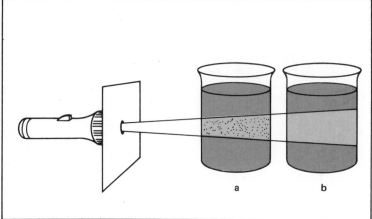

Figure G　　　　　　**Figure H**

One of these mixtures is a solution. The other is a colloid.

They both look the same until we shine a beam of light through them.

1. Beaker _____ shows the Tyndall effect.
   a, b

2. Beaker _____ does not show the Tyndall effect.
   a, b

3. The solution is in beaker _____ .
   a, b

4. The colloid is in beaker _____ .
   a, b

5. _____ particles are the size of molecules.
   Colloid, Solution

6. _____ particles are larger than molecules.
   Colloid, Solution

Figure I

Why do "quiet" lakes have clear water? _____

_____

_____

_____

_____

How can the parts of a suspension be separated? | 15 |

coagulation [koh-ag-yoo-LAY-shun]:   use of chemicals to make the particles in a suspension clump together

filtration [fil-TRAY-shun]:   separation of particles in a suspension by passing it through paper or other substances

LESSON 15 | How can the parts of a suspension be separated?

A cook drains off the cooking water from spaghetti. The wind makes dust fly in the air, but it settles. Spaghetti in water and dust in the air are both suspensions. In both examples, the parts of the suspension separated.

Many kinds of suspensions must be separated. Sometimes, nature separates the parts. Other times we must do it ourselves—or help nature along.

There are four ways to separate suspensions. They are **filtration** [fil-TRAY-shun], sedimentation [sed-uh-men-TAY-shun], spinning, and **coagulation** [koh-ag-yoo-LAY-shun].

FILTRATION Filtration is the same as straining. A filter has holes. Pieces smaller than the holes pass right through. Larger pieces are trapped by the filter.

Filters come in many sizes. Some have large holes. Some have small holes. The size of the filter you use depends upon the size of the particles you want to separate.

SEDIMENTATION Nature does this job itself. In sedimentation, the suspension just "sits." Gravity makes the pieces settle to the bottom of their containers.

SPINNING Spinning speeds settling. Spinning builds a strong outward force. The force pushes the pieces to the bottom of the container quickly.

COAGULATION Coagulation also speeds settling. Coagulation uses chemicals. The chemicals make small particles lump together. They become heavy and settle fast.

Coagulation occurs when you cut yourself. Chemicals in your blood cause the blood to coagulate and form a clot.

FILTRATION

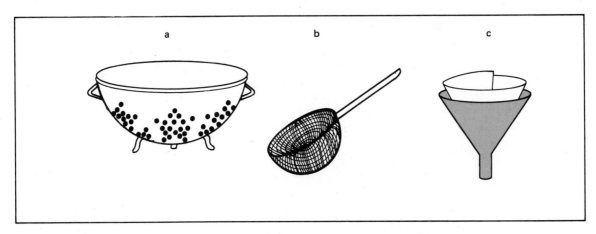

Figure A

1. Which filter separates out the largest pieces? _____

2. Which one separates out the smallest pieces? _____

3. Which filter would you use to strain spaghetti? _____

4. Does filtration use chemicals? _____

SEDIMENTATION

Figure B

1. In sedimentation:

    a) the heaviest pieces settle _____ .
    first, last

    b) the lightest particles settle _____ .
    first, last

2. Sedimentation is done by _____ .
    gravity, spinning

3. Does sedimentation use chemicals? _____

99

Figure C

There are suspensions of clay and water in the can and the beaker.

1. The clay pieces will settle first in the _____ .
    <small>beaker, can</small>

2. The pieces in the beaker are settling by _____ .
    <small>spinning, gravity</small>

3. The pieces in the can are settling by _____ .
    <small>spinning, gravity</small>

4. Spinning causes an _____ force.
    <small>outward, inward</small>

5. Spinning _____ settling.
    <small>speeds, slows</small>

6. Does spinning use chemicals? _____

COAGULATION

Figure D

1. The suspension in beaker b is settling by _____ .
   <u>coagulation, sedimentation</u>

2. Coagulation makes small particles _____ .
   <u>lump together, move apart</u>

3. Coagulated particles become _____ .
   <u>heavier, lighter</u>

4. Heavy particles settle more _____ than light ones.
   <u>slowly, quickly</u>

5. Coagulation uses _____ and then gravity.
   <u>spinning, chemicals</u>

WHEN ARE SUSPENSIONS SEPARATED?

You have learned four ways of removing particles from suspensions. These can be very useful. Here is one example.

Most places get their drinking water from rivers, lakes, or reservoirs. The water has sediment suspended in it. It must be removed so the water can be fit to drink.

Several steps are used to remove the sediment. You will learn about these steps in Lesson 21.

Figure E

Complete each statement using a term or terms from the list below. Write your answers in the spaces provided. Some words may be used more than once.

spinning	first	coagulation
last	chemicals	lump together
gravity	sedimentation	filtration
outward	speed up	does not

1. The four ways of separating the parts of a suspension are _____ ,

   _____ , _____ , _____ .

2. The method that separates a suspension by trapping particles is _____ .

3. In sedimentation, _____ makes the particles settle.

4. Heavy particles settle _____ .

5. Lightweight particles settle _____ .

6. Spinning and coagulation _____ settling.

7. Spinning builds an _____ force.

8. Spinning _____ use chemicals.

9. Coagulation uses _____ and then gravity to make particles settle.

10. Coagulation makes small pieces _____ .

MATCHING

Match each term in Column A with its description in Column B. Write the correct letter in the space provided.

Column A	**Column B**
_____ 1. gravity	a) causes strong outward force
_____ 2. filtration	b) do not dissolve
_____ 3. spinning	c) lumps particles together
_____ 4. suspension particles	d) pulls things down
_____ 5. coagulation	e) traps particles

TRUE OR FALSE

In the space provided, write "true" if the sentence is true. Write "false" if the sentence is false.

_____ 1. Suspended particles can be separated.

_____ 2. Filtration separates pieces by weight.

_____ 3. All filters are the same size.

_____ 4. Sedimentation uses gravity.

_____ 5. Spinning causes an inward force.

_____ 6. Spinning and coagulation speed sedimentation.

_____ 7. Filtration uses chemicals.

_____ 8. Spinning uses chemicals.

_____ 9. Sedimentation uses chemicals.

_____ 10. Coagulation uses chemicals.

WORD SCRAMBLE

Below are several scrambled words you have used in this Lesson. Unscramble the words and write your answers in the spaces provided.

1. NORFATILIT   _____

2. DOTRAWU   _____

3. NIPSNGIN   _____

4. TAGYVIR   _____

5. GALUNOTIAOC   _____

6. TATMENNIODESI   _____

7. CALCHEMSI   _____

COMPLETE THE CHART

*Complete the chart by filling in the missing information. Identify whether each statement describes separation of a suspension by **filtration, coagulation,** or **spinning,** by placing an X in the correct column.*

	Description	Filtration	Coagulation	Spinning
1.	Particles stick together.			
2.	Particles are caught on paper.			
3.	Motion causes particles to be pulled out of a suspension.			
4.	Chemicals are added to the suspension.			

REACHING OUT

After sediment from a suspension settles, how can you separate it from the liquid?

_____

_____

_____

_____

_____

What is a solution?

dissolve: go into solution
solute [SAHL-yoot]:   substance that is dissolved in a solvent
solution: mixture in which one substance is evenly mixed with another substance
solvent: substance in which a solute dissolves

LESSON 16 | What is a solution?

You can be a magician! Just add sugar to water and stir. Abracadabra! The sugar disappears!

But is the sugar really gone? No. The sugar and water just mix together. They mix completely. The sugar just seems to disappear.

Sugar and water together form a mixture. There are several kinds of mixtures. Sugar and water form a special kind of mixture. They form a liquid **solution.** There are many kinds of liquid solutions.

A liquid solution has two parts: a **solute** [SAHL-yoot] and a **solvent.** The solvent is always a liquid. The solute is what "disappears" in the solvent. The solute may be a solid, a gas, or another liquid.

A liquid solution is formed when the solute **dissolves.** The solute spreads out evenly throughout the solvent. The substance that dissolves is said to be soluble [SAHL-yoo-bul].

In the example of sugar and water, the water is the solvent. Water dissolves sugar. The sugar is the solute. Sugar is soluble in water.

There are many kinds of solvents. There are many kinds of solutes. There are many kinds of liquid solutions.

Remember, a mixture is a liquid solution only if the solute dissolves and spreads out evenly.

All the examples in Figures A, B, and C are liquid solutions.

Remember, there are three states of matter—solid, liquid, and gas.

Figure A

Figure B

Figure C

1. Name the states of matter in this liquid solution (Figure A).

   _____ and _____

2. The solute is the

   _____ .
   solid, liquid

3. The solvent is the

   _____ .
   solid, liquid

4. Name the states of matter of this liquid solution (Figure B).

   _____ and

   _____ .

5. The solute is the

   _____ .
   gas, liquid

6. The solvent is the

   _____ .
   gas, liquid

7. Na the states of matter of this liquid solution (Figure C).

   _____ and _____ .

NOTE: In solutions where all the parts are liquid, we usually do not name the solute and solvent.

COMPLETING SENTENCES

Choose the correct word or term for each statement. Write your choice in the spaces provided.

1. A liquid solution has at least one _____ .
   solid, liquid, gas

2. The solute in a liquid solution _____ .
   must be a gas, must be a solid, can be any state of matter

3. In solutions of liquids and solids or of liquids and gases, the solvent is always the

   _____ .
   solid, liquid, gas

4. In solutions of all liquids, we usually _____ name the solute and
   solvent.   do, do not

WHICH ARE LIQUID SOLUTIONS?

Ten mixtures you know are listed below. Some are liquid solutions, some are not. Think about each mixture, then fill in the boxes.

	Mixture	Do the substances dissolve? (Write YES or NO.)	If the substances dissolved, name the solute (or solutes).	name the solvent.
1.	sugar water			
2.	muddy water			
3.	salty water			
4.	pebbles in water			
5.	instant coffee drink			
6.	orange juice			
7.	oil and water			
8.	instant tea drink			
9.	ocean water			
10.	vegetable soup			

108

FILL IN THE BLANK

Complete each statement using a term or terms from the list below. Write your answers in the spaces provided. Some words may be used more than once.

mixture	liquid solution	sugar water
two	liquid	solvent
solid	gas	solute
soluble	water	

1. Different things close together make up a _____ .

2. A _____ is a special kind of mixture.

3. An example of a liquid solution is _____ .

4. A liquid solution has _____ main parts.

5. One part of a liquid solution is always a _____ .

6. The liquid part of a liquid solution is called the _____ .

7. The other part of a liquid solution can be a _____ , or a

   _____ , or a _____ .

8. The part of a liquid solution that mixes into the solvent is called the

   _____ .

9. A solute that dissolves in a solvent is said to be _____ .

10. Sugar is soluble in _____ .

MATCHING

Match each term in Column A with its description in Column B. Write the correct letter in the space provided.

Column A	Column B
_____ 1. mixture	a) means "able to dissolve"
_____ 2. solute	b) liquid part of a liquid solution
_____ 3. solvent	c) different things close together
_____ 4. liquid solution	d) a special kind of mixture
_____ 5. soluble	e) part of a solution that is dissolved

Be a detective! How can you tell if a mixture is a liquid solution? We will learn more in following Lessons. Meanwhile, see if you can figure out the clues.

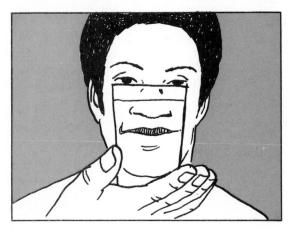

Figure D

• This is a mixture of muddy water

• Muddy water is not a liquid solution.

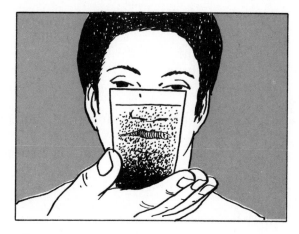

Figure E

• This is a mixture of sugar and water.

• Sugar and water is a liquid solution.

Answer YES or NO to these questions.

		Muddy Water	Sugar Water
1.	Are the parts evenly mixed?		
2.	Can you see the separate parts?		
3.	Do particles fall to the bottom?		
4.	Can you see clearly through this mixture?		

How can you tell if a mixture is a liquid solution?

In your own words, list the clues.

_____

_____

_____

_____

_____

What are the properties of solutions?

17

homogeneous [hoh-muh-JEE-nee-us]:   uniform; the same all the way through
properties [PROP-ur-tees]:   characteristics used to describe a substance
transparent [trans-PER-unt]:   material that transmits light easily

LESSON 17 | What are the properties of solutions?

What happens when you add salt to a jar of water and stir? The salt disappears. You have made a liquid solution. Does the same thing happen when you add sand to water? No. The sand settles to the bottom of the jar.

How can we tell if a mixture is a solution or not? We can tell by its **properties** [PROP-ur-tees]. Properties tell us how a kind of matter looks and acts.

These are the properties of liquid solutions:

(1) The parts dissolve and become the size of molecules.
(2) Liquid solutions are **homogenous** [hoh-muh-JEE-nee-us].
(3) Liquid solutions are **transparent** [trans-PER-unt].
(4) Liquid solutions do not settle out.

MOLECULE SIZE You know that matter is made up of tiny atoms. Most matter is made up of <u>groups</u> of atoms called molecules. In a liquid solution, the particles of solute dissolve. They break up until they are the size of molecules.

HOMOGENOUS Homogeneous means evenly mixed—the same all though. Because the particles are the size of molecules they weigh very little. They move around and spread out evenly.

TRANSPARENT You can see clearly through something that is transparent. Glass is transparent. So are liquid solutions. The molecules that make them up are tiny. They do not block out light. Light passes right through.

THE PARTS NEVER SETTLE OUT Something that settles out drops to the bottom of its container. The parts of a liquid solution never separate. They never settle out no matter how long they sit. That is because the molecules are light. They keep bouncing around. This also keeps the solution homogenous.

Figure A

Figure B

Look at Figure A.

1. Can you see the sugar particles? _____

yes, no

2. The sugar _____ dissolve.

did, did not

3. The sugar is now _____ .

the size of molecules, much larger than the size of molecules

4. Can the boy see through the sugar water? _____

yes, no

5. The sugar water is _____ .

cloudy, transparent

6. The mixture _____ evenly mixed.

is, is not

7. It _____ homogenous.

is, is not

8. The sugar _____ settling.

is, is not

9. Sugar water _____ a liquid solution.

is, is not

Look at Figure B.

1. Can you see the clay particles? _____

yes, no

2. The clay _____ dissolve.

did, did not

3. The clay particles are _____ .

the size of molecules, much larger than the size of molecules

113

4. Can the boy see clearly through the mixture? _____

yes, no

5. The clay water is _____ .

cloudy, transparent

6. The mixture _____ evenly mixed.

is, is not

7. It _____ homogenous.

is, is not

8. The clay _____ settling out.

is, is not

9. Clay water _____ a liquid solution.

is, is not

FILL IN THE BLANK

Complete each statement using a term or terms from the list below. Write your answers in the spaces provided. Some words may be used more than once.

liquid solutions	moving around	light
drop	is not	clay water
molecules	transparent	small in size

1. When we can look clearly through something we say it is _____ .

2. _____ are transparent.

3. _____ is not transparent.

4. Clay water _____ a liquid solution.

5. The parts of a liquid solution are the size of _____ .

6. The molecules of a liquid solution do not block _____ .

7. To "settle out" means to _____ .

8. The parts of _____ do not settle out.

9. Liquid solutions do not settle out because the parts are too

_____ .

10. The molecules in liquid solutions are always _____ .

WHICH IS HOMOGENOUS?

The dots stand for copper sulfate molecules. The liquid is water.

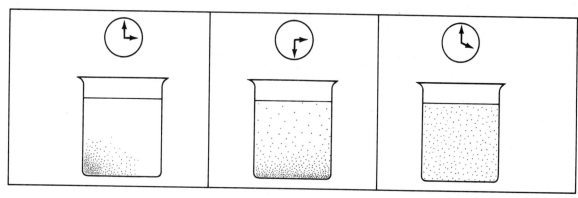

Figure C   **Figure D**   **Figure E**

1. Which figure shows a homogenous mixture? _____

2. a) The mixtures in Figures _____ and _____ are not liquid solutions.

   b) They are not liquid solutions because they _____ homogenous.
      <small>are, are not</small>

3. a) The mixtures that are not liquid solutions _____ become liquid solutions.
      <small>could, could not</small>

   b) They would be solutions if all the _____ dissolved, and spread out evenly.
      <small>solute, solvent</small>

4. Think about this: What would you do to make the mixtures that are not homogenous, become homogenous fast?

   _____

   _____

MATCHING

Match each term in Column A with its description in Column B. Write the correct letter in the space provided.

Column A	Column B
_____ 1. molecule	a) evenly mixed
_____ 2. homogenous	b) drop
_____ 3. settle out	c) tiny part of matter
_____ 4. properties	d) clear
_____ 5. transparent	e) things that help us identify matter

TRUE OR FALSE

In the space provided, write "true" if the sentence is true. Write "false" if the sentence is false.

_____ **1.** Anything we can see through clearly is transparent.

_____ **2.** Every mixture is homogenous.

_____ **3.** Sand becomes the size of molecules when it is in water.

_____ **4.** Liquid solutions are transparent.

_____ **5.** Muddy water is transparent.

_____ **6.** Muddy water settles out.

_____ **7.** The parts of liquids are the size of molecules.

_____ **8.** Salt water is a liquid solution.

_____ **9.** Liquid solutions settle out.

_____ **10.** The molecules of solutions are always moving around.

REACHING OUT

Transparent, translucent, and opaque are three words that have to do with light. Give a definition of each word in the spaces below. (You may use a dictionary.) Next to each definition give an example of each.

Transparent _____

_____

_____

Translucent _____

_____

_____

Opaque _____

_____

_____

Figure F

How can the strength of a solution be changed?

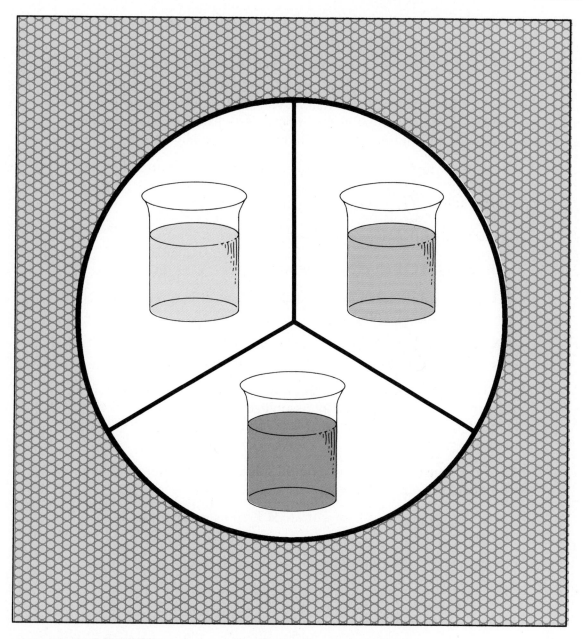

concentrated [KAHN-sun-trayt-ed] **solution:**   strong solution
dilute: [di-LEWT] **solution:**   weak solution
saturated [SACH-uh-rayt-id] **solution:**   solution containing all the solute it can hold at
   a given temperature

LESSON 18 | How can the strength of a solution be changed?

Some people like strong coffee. Others like it weak. What makes coffee strong or weak? You know that if you add more coffee it becomes stronger. If you add more water, it becomes weaker. A cup of coffee is like any liquid solution. It comes in many strengths.

We use these terms to describe how strong a liquid solution is:

- **dilute** [di-LEWT] **solution**

- **concentrated** [KAHN-sun-trayt-ed] **solution**

- **saturated** [SACH-uh-rayt-id] **solution:**

DILUTE A dilute solution is a weak solution. It has very little solute dissolved in the solvent.

CONCENTRATED A concentrated solution is a strong solution. It has more solute dissolved in it than a dilute solution has.

SATURATED A saturated solution is an extra-strong solution. It has so much solute that no more can dissolve. If we tried to add more solute, it would just drop to the bottom. More solute would dissolve only if the mixture were heated.

We can change the strength of a liquid solution. We do this by changing the amount of solute or solvent.

Terms like "dilute" and "concentrated" help us compare solutions.

A cup of instant tea is a liquid solution.

Two different cups of tea are shown in Figures A and B. Study them. Then fill in the blanks.

Figure A   **Figure B**

1. The instant tea _____ dissolve.

does, does not

2. A cup of tea _____ a liquid solution.

is, is not

3. In both solutions the solute is the _____ .

tea, water

4. In both solutions the solvent is the _____ .

tea, water

5. The cup of tea in Figure A has a _____ of solute compared to the solution in Figure B.

lot, little bit

6. The solution in Figure A is _____ than the solution in Figure B.

stronger, weaker

7. The solution in Figure A is more _____ than the solution in Figure B.

concentrated, dilute

8. The solution in Figure B _____ the same kind of solute and solvent as Figure A.

has, does not have

9. The amount of solvent is _____ in both solutions.
the same, different

10. The amount of solute is _____ in both solutions.
the same, different

11. There is _____ solute in Figure B.
more, less

12. This solution is _____ than the solution in Figure A.
stronger, weaker

13. This solution is _____ than the solution in Figure A.
more concentrated, more dilute

COLOR AND STRENGTH OF SOLUTIONS

Sometimes, color tells us about the strength of a solution. The darker the color, the stronger the solution. The lighter the color, the weaker the solution. We can use color only when we compare similar solutions.

Of Figures A and B on page 61:

1. which figure shows a darker solution? _____

2. which figure shows a lighter solution? _____

3. which solution is stronger? _____

4. which solution is weaker? _____

5. Why can color help us compare the strengths of these mixtures? _____

_____

_____

COMPARING CONCENTRATIONS

Figure C   **Figure D**   **Figure E**

Look at Figures C, D, and E. Each test tube contains a liquid solution. The kind of solute and solvent is the same in each.

1. Which is the strongest? _____

2. Which is the weakest? _____

3. Which has the most solute? _____

4. Which has the least solute? _____

5. Which one is closest to being saturated? _____

A SATURATED SOLUTION

Figure F

Figure G

The beakers in Figures F and G contain liquid solutions. The kind of solute and solvent is the same in each. Some additional solute has been added to each. Both mixtures have been stirred well.

1. Which is not saturated? _____

2. Which one is saturated? _____

3. How do you know? _____

_____

4. Take a guess! How can we make the extra solute dissolve? _____

_____

_____

FILL IN THE BLANK

Complete each statement using a term or terms from the list below. Write your answers in the spaces provided.

lighter
very little
color
dilute

strengths
raising the temperature
concentrated

saturated
a lot
darker

1. Liquid solutions come in different _____ .

2. A weak solution is called _____ .

3. A strong solution is called _____ .

4. Dilute solutions have _____ solute.

5. Concentrated solutions have _____ of solute.

6. A solution that can dissolve no more solute is called _____ .

7. We can make a saturated solution dissolve more solute by

   _____ .

8. Sometimes we can use _____ to compare the strengths of solutions.

9. In comparing strength by color, the _____ color, the stronger the solution.

10. In comparing strength by color, the _____ the color, the weaker the solution.

MATCHING

Match each term in Column A with its description in Column B. Write the correct letter in the space provided.

Column A	Column B
_____ 1. dilute solution	a) extra solvent does not dissolve
_____ 2. concentrated solution	b) more solute dissolves
_____ 3. saturated solution	c) strong solution
_____ 4. raising the temperature	d) sometimes used to compare solution strengths
_____ 5. color	e) weak solution

WORD SEARCH

The list on the left contains words that you have used in this Lesson. Find and circle each word where it appears in the box. The spellings may go in any direction: up, down, right, or diagonally.

MOLECULE

SOLUTE

SOLVENT

DILUTE

SOLUBLE

GAS

DISSOLVE

SOLID

MIXTURE

LIQUID

SATURATE

Y	M	I	X	T	U	R	E	D	C
R	S	O	L	U	T	E	U	I	L
A	O	S	L	I	D	V	N	S	O
G	L	T	N	E	V	L	O	S	S
E	U	D	M	P	C	S	L	O	E
T	B	R	I	T	X	U	E	L	L
A	L	U	L	L	S	D	L	V	B
R	E	S	E	O	U	A	M	E	I
U	D	O	A	B	E	T	A	P	C
T	D	L	Q	G	I	Z	E	R	S
A	U	I	L	E	S	L	I	E	I
S	Q	D	I	U	Q	I	L	A	M

REACHING OUT

Why can color be used only for comparing similar solutions and not for comparing different solutions?

_____

_____

_____

_____

SCIENCE *EXTRA*
Photography

Do you like to take pictures? Many people do. Photography is a great way to "capture" a scene and save it to look at some other time.

When most people have taken all the pictures on a roll of film, they drop the roll off at a supermarket or photography store to have the film developed. Some people, however, develop their own film. When you develop your own film, you have much more control of how the final photo will appear.

People usually learn how to develop black and white film before color film because black and white film is easier to develop. Light can ruin film so developing must be done in a dark room.

When you take a picture, light is let into the camera and forms an image on the film. The film is covered with silver salts that react to the light. The places that the light strikes are called exposed.

The first step in developing film is to treat the film with a chemical

called a developer. This chemical reacts with the exposed silver salts on the film to make silver. The film is then rinsed to stop the reaction.

Next, the film is treated with a chemical called a fixer which dissolves the unexposed silver salts. When the film is rinsed again, these silver salts wash away. Finally, the film is dried. The film is now called a negative.

The negatives are put into a device called an enlarger. The enlarger works like a slide projector. An image from the negative is projected onto special printing paper. This paper is treated with chemicals similar to the ones that were used to develop the film. You can make many photos of the same image. You can also make them any size you want to.

Developing your own photos is fun and can be less expensive as well. You can learn more about developing at a camera store or at your local library. So snap away.

How can solutes be made to dissolve faster?

19

LESSON 19 | How can solutes be made to dissolve faster?

What do you do after you add sugar to a drink? You stir. But why? You stir because you know that mixing makes sugar dissolve faster.

Stirring makes any solute dissolve faster.

Now here is another question. Which will dissolve faster, a lump of sugar or small grains of sugar? You know from experience that the smaller the pieces the faster it will dissolve.

Now let us tackle another question. Which will dissolve sugar faster, cold water or hot water?

From your experience you know that solutes dissolve faster in hot water.

There are three ways to make solids dissolve faster:

- <u>Stir the mixture.</u>

- <u>Break the solute into smaller pieces.</u>

- <u>Heat the mixture.</u>

Doing any of these things makes a solute dissolve faster. Doing two or all three dissolves the solute much faster.

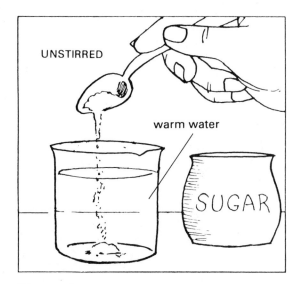

Figure A

Pour some granulated sugar into a glass of warm water. Do not stir.

Figure B

Pour the same amount of granulated sugar into another glass of warm water. Then stir.

Notice how fast the sugar dissolves in each glass.

1. Stirring makes a solute dissolve _____ .
faster, slower

Figure C

Pour some granulated sugar into cold water. Do not stir.

Figure D

Pour the same amount of granulated sugar into hot water. Do not stir.

Notice how fast the sugar dissolves in each beaker.

2. A solute dissolves faster in a _____ solvent.
hot, cold

3. A solute dissolves slower in a _____ solvent.
hot, cold

4. Heat makes a solute dissolve _____ .
slower, faster

Figure E

Figure F

Put a lump of sugar into a glass of hot water. Do not stir.

Pour one teaspoon of granulated sugar into a glass of hot water. Do not stir.

Notice how fast the sugar dissolves.

5. Big pieces dissolve _____ than small pieces.
slower, faster

6. Small pieces dissolve _____ than large pieces.
slower, faster

7. Crushing makes solutes dissolve _____ .
slower, faster

NOW TRY THESE

1. The two main parts of any liquid solution are the _____ and the

_____ .

2. The liquid part of a solution is called the _____ .

3. The part of a solution that dissolves into the liquid is called the

_____ .

4. Three ways we can make a solid solute dissolve faster are:

_____ ,_____ ,

and _____ .

COMPLETE THE CHART

Complete the chart by filling in the missing information.

	If you . . .	then the solute dissolves faster.	slower.
1.	make the pieces larger,		
2.	make the pieces smaller,		
3.	stir,		
4.	do not stir,		
5.	heat the solvent,		
6.	do not heat the solvent.		

TRUE OR FALSE

In the space provided, write "true" if the sentence is true. Write "false" if the sentence is false.

_____ **1.** Stirring moves things around.

_____ **2.** Crushing makes things larger.

_____ **3.** Heat lowers temperature.

_____ **4.** Stirring makes solutes dissolve faster.

_____ **5.** Small pieces of solute dissolve slower than big pieces.

_____ **6.** Heat makes solutes dissolve faster.

WORD SCRAMBLE

Below are several scrambled words you have used in this Lesson. Unscramble the words and write your answers in the spaces provided.

1. NEAHIGT _____

2. TARSEF _____

3. RIST _____

4. SCURH _____

5. SLEDSIVO _____

REACHING OUT

You put a piece of glass in water. It does not dissolve. You then crush it into tiny pieces.

Will the pieces dissolve? _____ Explain. _____

_____

_____

_____

_____

How can solutes change the freezing and boiling point of water?

20

LESSON 20

How can solutes change the freezing and boiling point of water?

Most automobile engines are cooled with water. In the winter, it is very cold in most parts of the country. If the water freezes, it can ruin the engine.

Car owners add antifreeze to the car's cooling system. This prevents the water from changing to ice. The same antifreeze also protects the engine from boiling over in the hot summer.

How does antifreeze work? Antifreeze acts like a solute in a solution. Putting antifreeze in the water of the cooling system raises the boiling point of the water. It also lowers the freezing point of the water.

Some dissolved solutes change the boiling and freezing point of water. Some dissolved solutes make it harder for water to freeze and boil.

This means that the water needs more cold to freeze and more heat to boil, The water freezes at a temperature lower than 0° C. It boils at a temperature higher than 100° C.

Adding more solutes lowers the freezing temperature and raises the boiling temperature even more. BUT THERE IS A LIMIT. After a certain amount of solute has been added, no more changes take place.

Certain solutes

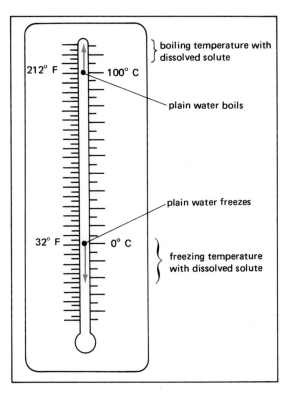

raise the boiling temperature,
        and
lower the freezing temperature of water.

Figure A

HOW DOES SALT CHANGE THE BOILING OF WATER?

What You Need (Materials)

2 beakers	water
2 ring stands and clamps	salt
2 thermometers	2 Bunsen burners

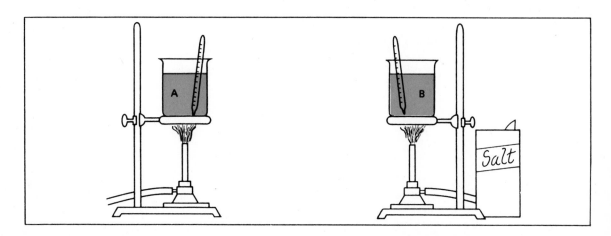

Figure B

How To Do The Experiment (Procedure)

1. Fill both beakers half full with water. Label one beaker A and the other B.

2. Stir a teaspoon of salt into beaker B only.

3. Set the beakers on the ringstands and place the thermometers in the water. **Light the burners.**

4. Observe the temperature at which the water boils in each beaker.

5. Put your observations on the chart below.

Boiling Point

PLAIN TAP WATER	
SALT WATER	

What You Learned (Observations)

1. The tap water boiled at _____° C.

2. The salt water boiled at _____° C.

3. The salt water boiled at a _____ temperature than the tap water.
   higher, lower

4. Water boils at a _____ temperature when a solute is added.
   higher, lower

Something To Think About (Conclusions)

1. Is salt water a solution? _____

2. Which part is the solute? _____

3. Which part is the solvent? _____

4. Do all dissolved solutes raise the boiling point of water? _____

Get two small plastic containers of the same size. Fill them half full with tap water.

Dissolve a tablespoon of salt into one of the containers.

Label this container S.

Place the containers in your freezer.

Check them every half hour.

Which one freezes first?

_____

_____

_____

Figure E

1. The plain tap water froze _____ than the salt water.
    <u>faster, slower</u>

2. The salt water froze _____ than the plain tap water.
    <u>faster, slower</u>

3. Dissolved salt water _____ to freeze.
    <u>easier, more difficult</u>

TRUE OR FALSE

In the space provided, write "true" if the sentence is true. Write "false" if the sentence is false.

_____ **1.** Adding solutes to water makes the water more difficult to freeze.

_____ **2.** Adding solutes to water lowers the freezing point.

_____ **3.** Adding solutes to water raises the freezing point.

_____ **4.** Adding solutes to water makes it easier to boil.

_____ **5.** Adding solutes to water raises the boiling point.

_____ **6.** Adding solutes to water lowers the boiling points.

_____ **7.** Antifreeze acts like a solute.

_____ **8.** The freezing point of plain water is higher than the freezing point of salt water.

_____ **9.** The boiling point of salt water is 100° C.

_____ **10.** The freezing point of plain water is 0° C.

REACHING OUT

Why do you think people put rock salt on icy sidewalks?

_____

_____

_____

_____

_____

_____

_____

Figure F

How can the parts of a solution be separated?

21

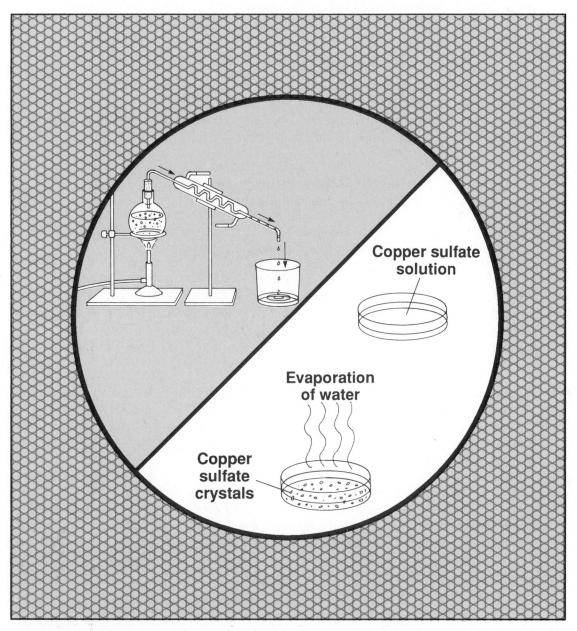

Copper sulfate solution

Evaporation of water

Copper sulfate crystals

condensation [kahn-dun-SAY-shun]:   change of a gas to a liquid
distillationn [dis-tuh-LAY-shun]:   process of evaporating a liquid and then condensing the gas back into a liquid
evaporation [i-vap-uh-RAY-shun]:   change of a liquid to a gas at the surface of the liquid

LESSON 21 | How can the parts of a solution be separated?

Everybody knows that ocean water tastes salty. Ocean water tastes salty because there is salt dissolved in it. Ocean water is a liquid solution. The water is the solvent. The salt is one of the solutes dissolved in it.

How can you prove that ocean water contains dissolved salt? Simple! Place some ocean water into a shallow dish and let it stand for a few days. Slowly the water disappears. The water changes to a gas and goes into the air. The salt stays behind as a solid.

The process of separating the salt from the sea is called **evaporation** [i-vap-uh-RAY-shun]. Evaporation is the change of a liquid to a gas. If you heat the solution, evaporation will occur faster.

Any liquid solution can be separated by evaporation, but only the solid solute will remain. The solvent escapes into the air.

What happens if you pass salt water through filter paper? Does the filter paper trap the salt? The answer is no! A liquid solution cannot be separated by filtering. Why not? The parts of a liquid solution are the size of molecules. They are so tiny that they pass right through the holes of the filter paper. The holes in filter paper are small, but the molecules are much smaller.

Another method of separating a solute from a solution is by **distillation** [dis-tuh-LAY-shun]. In the process of distillation, a liquid is heated until it evaporates. The gas is then cooled until it changes back into a liquid. The process by which gas changes back into a liquid is called **condensation** [kahn-dun-SAY-shun].

When a solution is distilled, both the solvent and the solute can be saved. The solution to be separated is heated. The solvent evaporates and forms a gas. The gas moves through a tube called a condenser. The condenser cools the gas back to a liquid. The liquid drips into a container. The solute remains in the original container. Both the solute and the solvent are saved.

A DISTILLATION UNIT

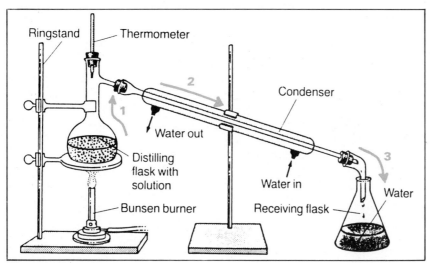

Figure C

How a Distillation Unit Works:

1. A solution is heated in a flask and the water turns to steam. Solids or liquids that have not reached their evaporation point remain the flask.

2. The steam enters the condenser and is cooled. As it cools, it changes back to a liquid.

3. The condensed liquid comes out of the condenser and enters the receiving flask.

WHAT HAPPENS IN DISTILLATION?

Check with Figure C as you read.

1. The liquid solution is boiled in the boiler. The solvent evaporates. The solvent

   changes from a _____ to a gas (water vapor).

2. The vapor moves out of the boiler. It goes into the inner tube of the cooling section.

3. The cold water in the outer tube cools the vapor. This makes the vapor condense.

   The vapor changes from a _____ back to a liquid.

4. The liquid drips into a container. It is pure. It has been distilled. It has no solute dissolved in it.

5. What happens to the solute? The solid solute stays behind in the boiler. It is now dried up. It is in solid form.

CAN FILTERING SEPARATE A SOLUTE FROM A SOLVENT?

What You Need (Materials)

2 beakers
copper sulfate solution
funnel
filter paper
ring stand

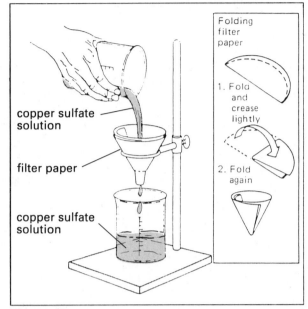

Figure B

How To Do the Experiment (Procedure)

1. Set up the ring stand with the funnel in place.

2. Fold the filter paper as shown in Figure B and place in the funnel.

3. Put the beaker under the funnel.

4. Pour the copper sulfate solution through the filter paper.

What You Learned (Observations)

1. The solute _____ left behind in the filter paper.
   _{was, was not}

2. The solvent _____ left behind in the filter paper.
   _{was, was not}

3. The solute particles are _____ than the holes in the filter paper.
   _{larger, smaller}

4. The solvent particles are _____ than the holes in the filter paper.
   _{larger smaller}

Something To Think About (Conclusions)

1. A liquid solution _____ be separated by filtering.
   _{can, cannot}

2. The parts of a liquid solution are _____.
   _{the size of molecules, larger than the size of molecules}

3. Filter paper holes are _____.
   _{the size of molecules, larger than the size of molecules}

140

A DISTILLATION UNIT

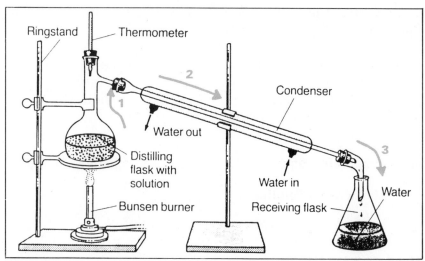

Figure C

How a Distillation Unit Works:

1. A solution is heated in a flask and the water turns to steam. Solids or liquids that have not reached their evaporation point remain the flask.

2. The steam enters the condenser and is cooled. As it cools, it changes back to a liquid.

3. The condensed liquid comes out of the condenser and enters the receiving flask.

WHAT HAPPENS IN DISTILLATION?

Check with Figure C as you read.

1. The liquid solution is boiled in the boiler. The solvent evaporates. The solvent

   changes from a _____ to a gas (water vapor).

2. The vapor moves out of the boiler. It goes into the inner tube of the cooling section.

3. The cold water in the outer tube cools the vapor. This makes the vapor condense.

   The vapor changes from a _____ back to a liquid.

4. The liquid drips into a container. It is pure. It has been distilled. It has no solute dissolved in it.

5. What happens to the solute? The solid solute stays behind in the boiler. It is now dried up. It is in solid form.

FILL IN THE BLANK

Complete each statement using a term or terms from the list below. Write your answers in the spaces provided. Some words may be used more than once.

filtering	distillation	drop
gas	larger	solvent
solute	heated	liquid
distilled		

1. When a liquid solution evaporates, only the _____ changes to a gas.

2. Evaporation happens faster when a solution is _____ .

3. Filter paper holes are _____ than the size of molecules.

4. Liquid solutions cannot be separated by _____ .

5. Evaporation saves only the _____ of a liquid solution.

6. _____ gets back both the solute and the solvent from a liquid solution.

7. In evaporation a _____ changes to a _____ .

8. In condensation a _____ changes to a _____ .

9. Condensation takes place when there is a _____ in temperature.

10. _____ water has no solutes in it.

WORD SCRAMBLE

Below are several scrambled words you have used in this Lesson. Unscramble the words and write your answers in the spaces provided.

1. NEDTASCONION   _____

2. TILLSIDNATION   _____

3. NIOTRAPAEOV   _____

4. LOTSUE   _____

5. THEA   _____

What are acids?

acid: substance that reacts with metals to release hydrogen
indicator [IN-duh-kayt-ur]: substance that changes color in acids and bases

LESSON 22 | What are acids?

The sour taste of the lemon juice tells us that it is an **acid**. Acids are special kinds of chemicals. They are common in everyday life. Some are helpful, others are harmful. There are some that are weak. Others are strong. Many acids are <u>dangerous</u> to touch or taste. You should <u>never</u> touch or taste an unknown acid.

Besides the sour taste that acids have, there are other tests for identifying them. Certain chemicals change color when acids are added.

Chemicals that change color are called **indicators** [IN-duh-kayt-urz].

An example of an indicator is a litmus paper. Litmus paper comes in two colors, red and blue.

Acids turn blue litmus paper red. Acids do not change the color of red litmus paper.

When acids mixed with metals a chemical reaction takes place. Hydrogen gas is given off from this reaction.

TESTING FOR AN ACID

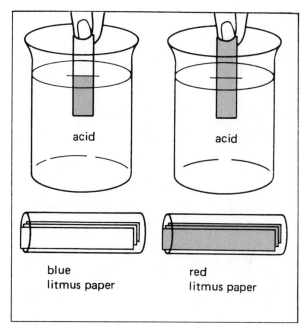

Acids turn blue litmus paper red.

Does the red litmus paper change color

with acids? _____

Figure A

SOME COMMON ACIDS

The chart lists some common acids and their chemical formulas. It shows you what all acids have in common. All acids contain the element hydrogen (H+).

	ACID	CHEMICAL FORMULA	USES
1.	Acetic acid	$HC_2H_3O_2$	vinegar
2.	Boric acid	H_3BO_3	eyewash
3.	Carbonic acid	H_2CO_3	club soda
4.	Citric acid	$H_3C_6H_5O_7$	citrus fruits
5.	Hydrochloric acid	HCl	aids digestion
6.	Nitric acid	HNO_3	fertilizers
7.	Sulfuric acid	H_2SO_4	plastics

Figure B *Citrus fruits have an acid called citric acid.*

Figure C *Vinegar is acetic acid.*

Figure D *Sulfuric acid is used in car batteries.*

Figure E *Hydrochloric acid produced in the stomach helps in digestion.*

FILL IN THE BLANK

Complete each statement using a term or terms from the list below. Write your answers in the spaces provided. Some words may be used more than once.

never	acid	blue
vinegar	hydrochloric acid	red
litmus paper	hydrogen	citric
dangerous		

1. Lemons contain _____ acid.

2. _____ is a kind of indicator.

3. Acids turn _____ litmus paper red.

4. _____ litmus paper does not change color in acids.

5. When acids wear away metals, _____ is given off.

6. Acetic acid is found in household _____ .

7. Your stomach produces_____ .

8. All acids contain the element _____ .

9. Some acids are _____ to touch or taste.

10. You should _____ touch or taste an _____ .

TRUE OR FALSE

In the space provided, write "true" if the sentence is true. Write "false" if the sentence is false.

_____ 1. Litmus paper is an indicator.

_____ 2. Acids turn red litmus paper blue.

_____ 3. Acids contain hydrogen.

_____ 4. Acids wear away metals.

_____ 5. Oxygen is given off when acids wear down metals.

WORD SCRAMBLE

Below are several scrambled words you have used in this lesson. Unscramble the words and write your answers in the spaces provided.

1. CADI _____

2. TRINOCDIA _____

3. SSTTE _____

4. SITLUM _____

5. RUSO _____

REACHING OUT

Figure F

Sometimes when rain falls, it mixes with pollution particles in the air. An acid is formed.

Why might this be harmful? _____

_____

_____

_____

What are bases?

23

base: substance formed when metals react with water

phenolphthalein [fee-nohl-THAL-een]: an indicator that turns a deep pink color when a base is added

LESSON 23 | What are bases?

Bases are a group of chemicals that have certain properties. Their properties are different from the properties of acids. Often they act <u>opposite</u> to the ways that acids act.

However, like acids, bases may be of different strengths. Some are very weak. Some are very strong. Some bases are dangerous to touch or taste. You should <u>never</u> touch or taste an unknown base.

Let us see how bases act with tests that we use to identify chemicals.

Bases have a <u>bitter taste</u>.

If you touch a harmless base it will <u>feel slippery</u>. Acids do not have any special feel.

Bases act the opposite way from acids with indicators. Bases turn <u>red litmus paper blue</u>. They do not change blue litmus paper.

There is another indicator that helps us to identify bases. It is called **phenolphthalein** [fee-nohl-THAL-een]. This solution is clear in acids. But phenolphthalein turns deep pink in bases.

Unlike acids, bases do not wear away metals.

TESTING FOR A BASE

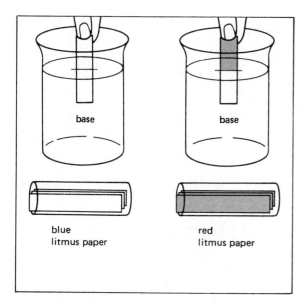

Figure A

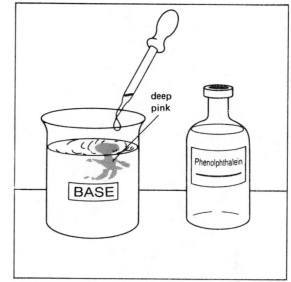

Figure B

Bases turn red litmus paper blue. Blue litmus paper does not change color.

What happens to blue litmus paper in acids? _____

Phenolphthalein turns deep pink in bases.

What happens to phenolphthalein in acids?

_____

SOME COMMON BASES

The chart lists some common bases and their chemical formulas It shows you what all bases have in common. All bases contain special groups of oxygen and hydrogen atoms called hydroxides (OH⁻).

	BASE	CHEMICAL FORMULA	USES
1.	Potassium hydroxide	KOH	soap
2.	Magnesium hydroxide	$Mg(OH)_2$	milk of magnesia
3.	Calcium hydroxide	$Ca(OH)_2$	mortar
4.	Ammonium hydroxide	NH_4OH	ammonia
5.	Sodium hydroxide	$NaOH$	soap

Figure C *Ammonia is used in cleaning products.*

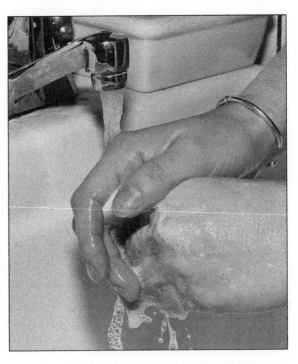

Figure D *Soap contains a base called lye.*

Figure E *Milk of magnesia is used to neutralize excess stomach acids.*

Figure F *Ammonium hydroxide is important in making fertilizers.*

FILL IN THE BLANK

Complete each statement using a term or terms from the list below. Write your answers in the spaces provided.

bitter   dangerous   opposite to
chemicals do not change pink
change   indicators   sour
lye

1. Bases are a group of _____ .

2. Bases often act_____ the ways that acids act.

3. Both acids and bases can be _____ .

4. Bases have a _____ taste.

5. Acids have a _____ taste.

6. Bases _____ the color of red litmus paper.

7. Bases _____ the color of blue litmus paper.

8. Phenolphthalein turns _____ in bases.

9. Phenolphthalein and litmus paper are _____ .

10. Soap contains a base called _____ .

MATCHING

Match each term in Column A with its description in Column B. Write the correct letter in the space provided.

	Column A	Column B
_____	1. red litmus paper	a) ammonia
_____	2. blue litmus paper	b) turns pink in bases
_____	3. phenolphthalein	c) turns blue in bases
_____	4. an acid	d) stays blue in bases
_____	5. a base	e) vinegar

TRUE OR FALSE

In the space provided, write "true" if the sentence is true. Write "false" if the sentence is false.

_____   1. Bases taste sour.

_____   2. Bases feel slippery.

_____   3. Bases turn blue litmus paper red.

_____   4. Bases turn red litmus paper blue.

_____   5. Phenolphthalein turns deep pink in bases.

_____   6. Bases wear away metals.

_____   7. Bases can be dangerous.

_____   8. Acids contain the OH^- groups.

_____   9. Acids contain the H^+ groups.

_____   10. All bases are strong.

REACHING OUT

Why are indicators useful? _____

_____

_____

What happens when acids and bases are mixed?

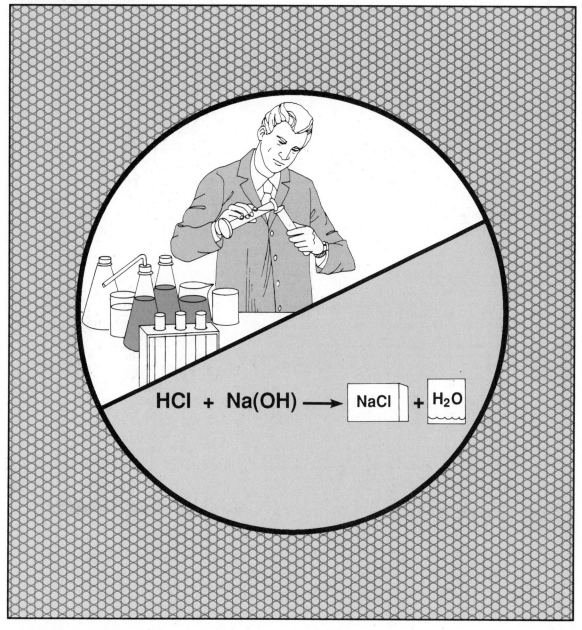

24

$$HCl + Na(OH) \longrightarrow NaCl + H_2O$$

neutral: neither acidic nor basic
neutralization [new-truh-li-ZAY-shun]: reaction between an acid and a base to produce a salt and water

LESSON 24 | What happens when acids and bases are mixed?

In chemistry, a liquid is **neutral** if it is not an acid nor a base. Take water, for example. Water is neutral. It is not an acid. It is not a base.

Acids and bases have definite properties. In many ways they are opposite What happens if you mix an acid with a base?

When you mix an acid with a base, a chemical reaction takes place. The atoms from the acid and the base change the way they are linked up. New products are formed. These new products have their own properties. The properties are different from the properties of either acids or bases.

What do you get?

When you mix the right amounts of an acid and a base, you get a salt and water. The salt is dissolved in the water. It forms a salt solution. A salt solution is not an acid: it is not a base. It is neutral.

$$\text{ACID + BASE} \xrightarrow{\text{makes}} \text{SALT + WATER}$$

The link-up of an acid and a base to form a salt and water is called **neutralization** [new-truh-li-ZAY-shun].

There are many kinds of salts. The salt you sprinkle on your food is just one kind of salt called sodium chloride. Its formula is NaCl. Different salts have different formulas.

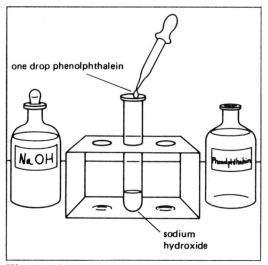

Figure A

The test tube in Figure A contains twenty drops of sodium hydroxide (NaOH).

One drop of phenolphthalein is added. The phenolphthalein turns deep pink.

This shows that sodium hydroxide (NaOH)

is _____ .

an acid, a base

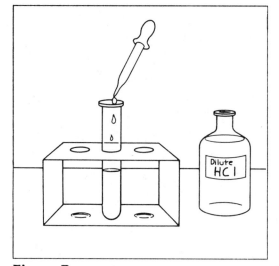

Figure B

A different dropper is used in Figure B to add fifteen drops of hydrochloric acid (HCl) — one drop at a time.

The solution stays pink.

This show that the solution

_____ .

is neutral, is an acid, is still a base

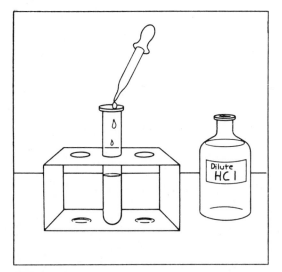

Figure C

More hydrochloric acid (HCl) is added — one drop at a time, until the pink disappears.

The loss of the pink color shows that the

solution is _____ .

an acid, no longer a base

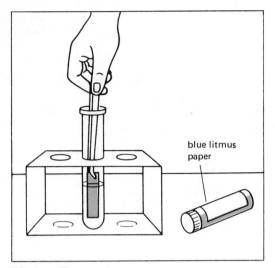

Figure D

The solution is tested with blue litmus paper.

The blue litmus paper stays blue.

This shows that the solution is not

_____ .
an acid, a base

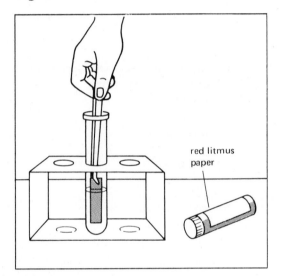

Figure E

The solution is tested with red litmus paper.

The red litmus paper stays red.

This shows that the solution is

_____ .
an acid, a base

The mixture _____ neutral.
is, is not

Fill in the boxes to show what happened:

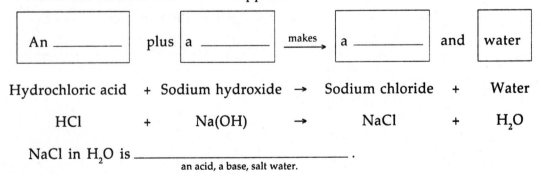

Hydrochloric acid + Sodium hydroxide → Sodium chloride + Water

HCl + Na(OH) → NaCl + H₂O

NaCl in H₂O is _____ .
an acid, a base, salt water.

FILL IN THE BLANK

Complete each statement using a term or terms from the list below. Write your answers in the spaces provided. Some words may be used more than once.

water	a base	table
neutralization	many kinds	neutral
litmus paper	reaction	phenolphthalein
an acid	a salt	

1. Lemon juice is an example of _____ . Lye is an example of

    _____ .

2. Any substance that is not an acid nor a base is said to be _____ .

3. An example of a neutral liquid is _____ .

4. The mixing of an acid and a base causes a chemical _____ .

5. If we mix the right amounts of an acid and a base, we get _____ and

    _____ .

6. The chemical reaction between an acid and a base to produce a salt and water is

    called _____ .

7. There are _____ of salts.

8. The most common salt is _____ salt.

9. Salt water does not change the color of _____

    or _____ .

10. Salt water is neither _____ nor _____ . Salt water is

    _____ .

MATCHING

Match each term in Column A with its description in Column B. Write the correct letter in the space provided.

	Column A		Column B
_____	1. HCI	a)	acid
_____	2. NaOH	b)	water
_____	3. H_2O	c)	base
_____	4. NaCl	d)	indicator
_____	5. phenolphthalein	e)	salt

TRUE OR FALSE

In the space provided, write "true" if the sentence is true. Write "false" if the sentence is false.

_____   1. An acid is neutral.

_____   2. A base is neutral.

_____   3. Water is neutral.

_____   4. There is only one formula for water.

_____   5. There is only one kind of salt.

_____   6. Salt water is neutral.

_____   7. If you mix an acid with a base, you get only water

_____   8. Blue litmus paper changes to red in salt water.

_____   9. Red litmus paper stays red in salt water.

_____   10. Phenolphthalein turns pink in salt water.

REACHING OUT

When hydrochloric acid reacts with potassium hydroxide, potassium chloride is formed.

• The formula for hydrochloric acid is HCl.

• The formula for potassium hydroxide is KOH.

What is the formula for water? _____

What is the formula for potassium chloride? _____

Why do some liquids conduct electricity?

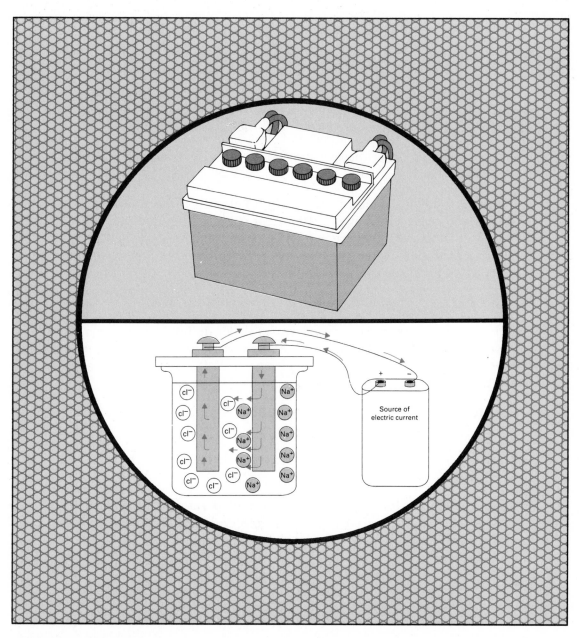

electrolyte [i-LEK-truh-lyt]: substance that conducts an electric current when it is dissolved in water

ion [Y-un]: charged particle

LESSON 25 | Why do some liquids conduct electricity?

Solutions of acids, bases, and salts conduct electricity. Solid acids, bases, and salts do not. Neither do liquids like alcohol, sugar water, distilled water, and glycerine.

Why do liquid acids, bases, and salts conduct electricity? Scientists explain it this way.

Matter is made up of atoms and groups of atoms called molecules. Most atoms and molecules have no electrical charge. They are neutral. The atoms of substances that are not acids, bases, or salts stay neutral. They stay neutral even when they dissolve. Solutions of acids, bases, and salts do not stay neutral.

What happens to an acid, base, or salt when it dissolves?

When an acid, base, or salt dissolves, its atoms do not stay together. The atoms unlock. When thy unlock, they do not stay neutral. They take on electrical charges. Some atoms have a positive (+) charge. Some have a negative (–) charge. Charged atoms are called **ions** [Y-unz].

Ions let electricity pass through a solution. Solutions that have ions are called **electrolytes** [i-LEK-truh-lyts].

Liquid acids, bases, and salts form ions. That is why they conduct electricity.

Liquids such as alcohol, sugar water, distilled water, and glycerine do not form ions. That is why they do not conduct electricity. They are nonelectrolytes.

We can test whether a solution conducts electricity by using a battery and a light bulb. The bulb lights up if the liquid is an electrolyte.

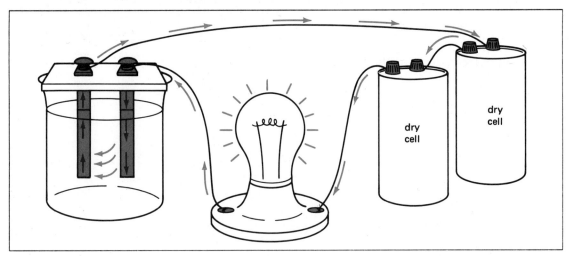

Figure A

The brightness of the light tells if the electrolyte is strong or weak.

- A <u>bright</u> light means a <u>strong electrolyte</u> (good conductor).
- A <u>dim</u> light means a <u>weak electrolyte</u> (poor conductor).
- <u>No</u> light means a <u>nonelectrolyte</u> (nonconductor).

The chart below lists 10 liquids. They have been tested as in Figure A. The checks show how brightly the bulb lit up.

	Liquid	Light Brightness		
		Bright	**Dim**	**No Light**
1.	Sodium chloride (salt)			
2.	Sugar			
3.	Boric acid			
4.	Sodium hydroxide (base)			
5.	Distilled water			
6.	Acetic acid			
7.	Alcohol			
8.	Magnesium sulfate (salt)			
9.	Glycerine			
10.	Carbonic acid			

Answer these questions about the information on the chart.

1. List the electrolytes _____

    _____

    _____

2. **a)** Which are strong electrolytes? _____

    _____

    _____

    b) How do you know? _____

3. **a)** Which are weak electrolytes? _____

    _____

    b) How do you know? _____

4. **a)** Which are nonelectrolytes? _____

    _____

    b) How do you know? _____

5. Which groups of liquids let the bulb light up? _____

    _____

6. Which groups of liquids are electrolytes? _____

    _____

TRUE OR FALSE

In the space provided, write "true" if the sentence is true. Write "false" if the sentence is false.

_____ 1. A regular atom has a charge.

_____ 2. An ion has a charge.

_____ 3. Only positive ions have a charge.

_____ 4. Liquids that conduct electricity are called electrolytes.

_____ 5. Electrolytes contain ions.

_____ 6. An electrolyte contains plus and minus ions.

164

Let us see what happens in a salt solution.

Table salt has atoms of sodium (Na) and chlorine (Cl). One molecule of salt has one atom of sodium linked to one atom of chlorine. Atoms of sodium and chlorine have no charge. Molecules of the solid salt NaCl have no charge

NaCl in the solid state does not conduct electricity.

When NaCl dissolves, the sodium and chlorine atoms break away from each other. They take on electrical charges. The sodium takes on a positive charge. The chlorine takes on a negative charge.

The charged atoms are now called ions. Ions conduct electricity. Liquids that form ions are called electrolytes.

- Liquid acids, bases, and salts form ions.

- Liquid acids, bases, and salts are electrolytes.

- Liquid acids, bases, and salts conduct electricity.

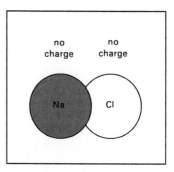

Figure B *One molecule of salt in the solid state*

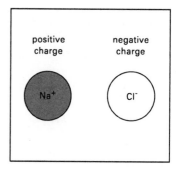

Figure C *One molecule of salt in the ionized state*

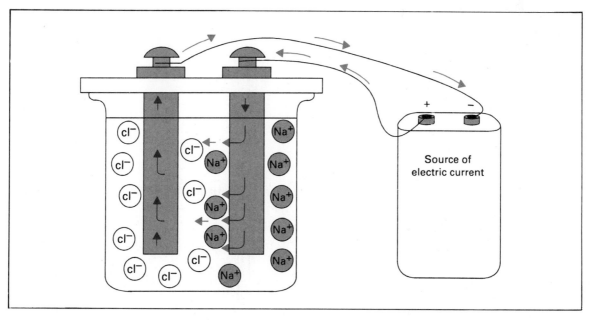

Figure D

FILL IN THE BLANK

Complete each statement using a term or terms from the list below. Write your answers in the spaces provided. Some words may be used more than once.

salts   electrolytes   negative
positive   no   atoms
ions   bases   conduct
acids

1. Matter that is electrically neutral has _____ charge.

2. Regular _____ are electrically neutral.

3. Regular atoms have _____ charge.

4. Atoms that have a charge are called _____ .

5. Some ions have a _____ charge; some have a _____ charge.

6. Atoms of _____ , _____ , and _____ form ions.

7. Ions _____ electricity.

8. Solutions that conduct electricity are called _____ .

9. Liquid _____ , _____ , and _____ are electrolytes.

10. Liquids like alcohol and distilled water do not form _____ . They are

    not _____ .

MATCHING

Match each term in Column A with its description in Column B. Write the correct letter in the space provided.

Column A	Column B
_____ 1. ion	a) kinds of charges
_____ 2. positive and negative	b) do not conduct electricity
_____ 3. electrolyte	c) liquid that conducts electricity
_____ 4. regular atom	d) charged atom or molecule
_____ 5. dry acids, bases, and salts	e) has no charge

What are oxidation numbers?

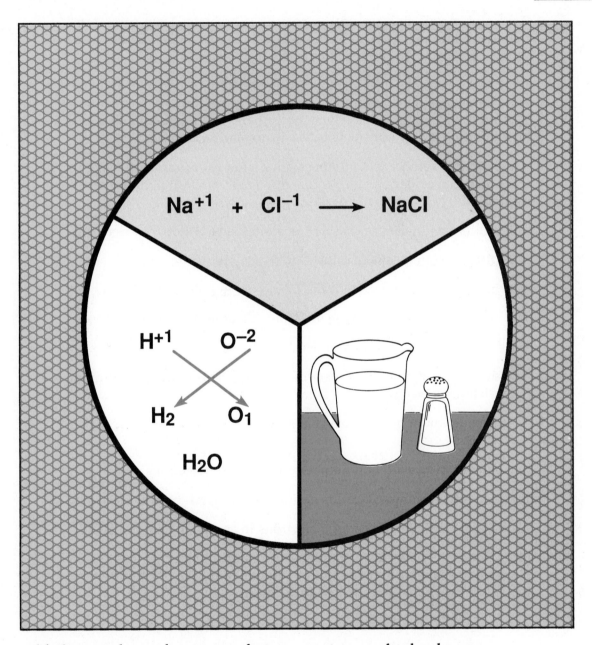

26

$$Na^{+1} \ + \ Cl^{-1} \longrightarrow NaCl$$

$$H^{+1} \qquad O^{-2}$$

$$H_2 \qquad O_1$$

$$H_2O$$

oxidation numbers: how many electrons an atom can lend or borrow

LESSON 26 | What are oxidation numbers?

Atoms of metals link up with atoms of nonmetals. They form compounds. When a compound forms, the metal lends outer-ring electrons to the nonmetal. The nonmetal borrows the electrons.

How many electrons does an atom lend or borrow? It depends upon the atom. It also depends upon the compound being formed. Some atoms give up or take on more electrons than others. The number of electrons an atom can lend or borrow is called its **oxidation number**.

An oxidation number is a number with a plus (+) or minus (–) sign in front of it. The oxidation number is written next to the atom it describes, such as Al^{+3}, Mg^{+2}, Br^{-1}, and Se^{-2}.

The sign (+ or –) tells us whether the atom lends or borrows electrons.

• A <u>plus (+) sign</u> means that the atom <u>lends</u> electrons.

• A <u>minus (–) sign</u> means that the atom <u>borrows</u> electrons.

The number tells us <u>how many</u> electrons the atom lends or borrows.

Let's look at two oxidation numbers.

• Sodium has a oxidation number of +1 (Na^{+1}). This means that sodium can lend one electron.

• The oxidation number of oxygen is –2 (O^{-2}). Oxygen can borrow two electrons.

Metals have plus oxidation numbers. Metals lend electrons.

Nonmetals have minus oxidation numbers. Nonmetals borrow electrons.

A nonmetal will borrow enough electrons to complete its outer shell.

Many elements have more than one oxidation number. In fact, some elements have both plus and minus oxidation numbers. Sometimes they lend electrons. Sometimes they borrow electrons.

You can find the oxidation numbers of many elements by looking at the periodic table.

FINDING THE OXIDATION NUMBER OF A METAL

This is the simplest oxidation number to find. In many cases, the oxidation number of a metal is the same as the number of electrons in its outer shell.

A metal lends (loses) electrons. Therefore, its oxidation number is plus (+).

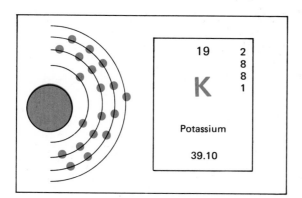

Figure A shows an example.

Potassium has 1 outer-shell electron.

Potassium lends this single electron.

The oxidation number of potassium is +1 (K^{+1}).

Figure A

FINDING THE OXIDATION NUMBER OF A NONMETAL

This is simple too. Here is what to do:

• Check the number of electrons in the outer shell.

• Figure out how many electrons that atom needs to make a stable outer shell (in most cases, 8 electrons). That number is the oxidation number.

A nonmetal will add, or borrow, these electrons. Therefore, its oxidation number is minus (–).

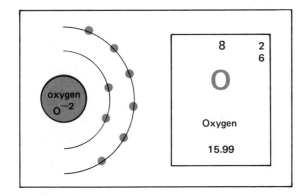

Figure B shows an example.

Oxygen has 6 outer-shell electrons.

Oxygen needs 2 more electrons to make its outer shell stable (8 – 6 = 2).

Oxygen will borrow (gain) these 2 electrons.

The oxidation number of oxygen is –2 (O^{-2}).

Figure B

4	2
	2

Be

Beryllium
9.01

Figure C

1. How many outer-shell electrons does beryllium have? _____

2. Beryllium is a _____ .

metal, nonmetal

3. Beryllium _____ electrons.

lends, borrows

4. How many electrons can beryllium lend? _____

5. What is the oxidation number of beryllium? _____

16	2
	8
	6

S

Sulfur

32.06

Figure D

6. a) How many outer-shell electrons does sulfur have? _____

   b) Is this a stable shell? _____

   c) How many electrons are needed to make a stable shell? _____

7. Sulfur is a _____ .

metal, nonmetal

8. Sulfur _____ electrons.

lends, borrows

9. How many electrons can sulfur borrow? _____

10. What is the oxidation number of sulfur? _____

WORKING WITH OXIDATION NUMBERS

Ten elements and their oxidation numbers are listed below. Study each one. Then fill in the chart. The first line has been filled in for you.

	Element	Symbol and oxidation number	Metal or nonmetal	Lends or borrow electrons?	Lends or borrows how many electrons?
1.	Oxygen	O^{-2}	Nonmetal	borrows	2
2.	Calcium	Ca^{+2}			
3.	Aluminum	Al^{+3}			
4.	Bromine	Br^{-1}			
5.	Nitrogen	N^{-3}			
6.	Zinc	Zn^{+2}			
7.	Lithium	Li^{+1}			
8.	Sulfur	S^{-2}			
9.	Phosphorus	P^{-3}			
10.	Silver	Ag^{+1}			

USING OXIDATION NUMBERS TO FIND FORMULAS

You can use oxidation numbers to figure out the formula for any simple compound. All you need to know are the symbols and the oxidation numbers of the elements that make up the compound. JUST CRISS-CROSS THE OXIDATION NUMBERS.

Water is made up of hydrogen (H) and oxygen (O). The oxidation number of hydrogen is +1 (H^{+1}). The oxidation number of oxygen is –2 (O^{-2}).

For example, this is how to write the formula for water:

Step 1   Write down the symbol of each element. List the element with the plus (+) oxidation number first.

H   O

Step 2   Write down the oxidation number of each element next to the element like this:

H^+ O^{-2}

Step 3   Criss-cross the <u>numbers</u> in the oxidation number only. Leave out the signs.

H^{+1} O^{-2}

H_2 O_1 = H_2O_1

One molecule of water, then, contains 2 atoms of hydrogen and 1 atom of oxygen.

In a final formula, we do not write any 1's. So the formula for water is H_2O.

Table salt is made up of atoms of sodium (Na) and chlorine (Cl). The oxidation number of sodium is +1 (Na^{+1}). The oxidation number of chlorine is –1 (Cl^{-1}).

Write it down. $Na^{+1}Cl^{-1}$

Cross over the numbers. $Na^{+1}Cl^{-1}$
                           Na_1Cl_1

Cancel out the ones. Na_xCl_y

The formula for table salt is **NaCl**.

Table salt is sodium chloride. One molecule of sodium chloride has 1 atom of sodium and 1 atom of chlorine. Altogether one molecule of salt contains 2 atoms.

What do you do if both oxidation numbers (not the signs) are the same? This is the case when magnesium and oxygen combine.

$$Mg^{+2}O^{-2}$$
$$Mg_2O_2 = Mg_2O_2$$

Cancel out both numbers like this: Mg_2O_2.

The formula, then is **MgO**.

There are some compounds where the numbers are not canceled out, but these compounds will not be covered in this book.

WRITING FORMULAS

Work these out by yourself. It's easy! Just do one step at a time.

Calcium (Ca) links up with iodine (I) to form a compound called calcium iodide.

The oxidation number of calcium is +2 (Ca^{+2}). The oxidation number of iodine is –1 (I^{-1}).

1. Write down each element and its oxidation number. (Remember, the + oxidation number comes first.)

   1. [ ]

2. Cross over the numbers.

   2. [ ]

3. Cancel out numbers. (Skip if not needed.)

   3. [ ]

4. Write the formula.

   4. [ ]

5. What is the name of this compound? _____

6. One molecule of calcium iodide has _____ atom(s) of calcium and

   _____ atom(s) of iodine.

7. Altogether, how many atoms does one molecule of calcium iodide have? _____

Gold and sulfur combine to form the compound gold sulfide.

The oxidation number of gold is +1 (Au^{+1}). The oxidation number of sulfur is –2 (S^{-2}).

8. Write down each element and its oxidation number.

   8. [ ]

9. Cross over numbers.

   9. [ ]

10. Cancel out numbers. (Skip if not needed.).

    10. [ ]

11. Write the formula.

    11. [ ]

12. What is the name of this compound? _____

13. One molecule of gold sulfide has _____ atom(s) of gold and

    _____ atom(s) of sulfur.

14. Altogether, how many atoms does one molecule of gold sulfide have? _____

Complete each statement using a term or terms from the list below. Write your answers in the spaces provided. Some words may be used more than once.

lend	oxidation number	number
more than one	borrow	stable outer shell
how many	loses	compounds
+ or – sign	gains	

1. Metals link up with nonmetals to form _____ .

2. When forming compounds, metals _____ electrons. Nonmetals

   _____ electrons.

3. An atom's _____ tells how many electrons the atom can lend or borrow.

4. A oxidation number is written as a _____ with a _____ in front of it.

5. The number tells us _____ electrons an atom gains or loses.

6. The sign tells us whether the atom will _____ or _____ electrons.

7. A atom with a plus (+) oxidation number lends electrons. Another way of saying

   this is: An atom with a plus oxidation number _____ electrons.

8. An atom with a minus (–) oxidation number borrows electrons. Another way of

   saying this is: An atom with a minus oxidation number _____ electrons.

9. A nonmetal will borrow enough electrons to give a _____ .

10. Many elements have _____ oxidation number.

MATCHING

Match each term in Column A with its description in Column B. Write the correct letter in the space provided.

Column A

_____ 1. compound

_____ 2. 2, 8, or 18 outer-shell electrons

_____ 3. oxidation number

_____ 4. + oxidation number atom

_____ 5. – oxidation number atom

Column B

a) tells how many electrons an atom can lend or borrow

b) lends electrons

c) at least one metal and one nonmetal

d) borrows electrons

e) stable outer shell

COMPLETE THE CHART

Write the correct formulas in the spaces below. Three formulas have been written for you.

NONMETALS

METALS		Cl^{-1}	S^{-2}	O^{-2}	I^{-1}	Br^{-1}
	H^{+1}	1. HCl	2.	3. H_2O	4.	5.
	Al^{+3}	6.	7.	8.	9. AlI_3	10.
	Ca^{+2}	11.	12.	13.	14.	15.
	Cu^{+1}	16.	17.	18.	19.	20.
	Mg^{+2}	21.	22.	23.	24.	25.
	Na^{+1}	26.	27.	28.	29.	30.

REACHING OUT

Oxidation numbers can help you find a formula. It goes the other way too. A formula can help you find the oxidation number of the elements in a compound.

For example, NiI_2 is the formula for nickel iodide. The formula tells us that:

- The oxidation number of nickel is +2. (Remember, the metal always goes first—and a metal has a positive (+) oxidation number.)

- The oxidation number of iodine is –1.

Six compounds are listed below. Figure out the oxidation number of the elements in each compound. The first one has been done for you.

	Formula	Atoms and Their Oxidation Numbers	
1.	CaF_2	Ca^{+2}	F^{-1}
2.	KBr		
3.	Mg_3N_2		
4.	CCl_4		
5.	H_2S		
6.	$FeCl_3$		

What is a polyatomic ion?

27

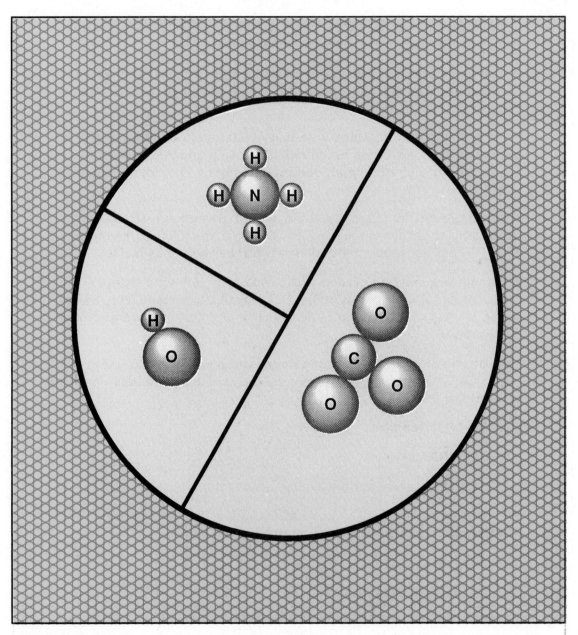

polyatomic [PAHL-i-uh-tahm-ik] **ion:** group of atoms that acts as a single atom
subscript: number written to the lower right of a chemical symbol

LESSON 27 | What is a polyatomic ion?

Many friends are "extra" good friends. They get together very often. And then, they seem to act like one person.

Certain elements are like that. They "get together" whenever possible. And then, they act as if they were one element.

A group of atoms that behaves like a single atom is called a **polyatomic** [PAHL-i-uh-tahm-ik] **ion** A polyatomic ion has its own oxidation number.

Eight common radicals along with their oxidation number are listed on the facing page. All the common radicals have a minus oxidation number except one. The ammonium radical (NH_4) has a +1 oxidation number $(NH_4)^{+1}$.

The radicals in the chart are listed within parenthesis like (OH). A parenthesis is not always needed. For example, the (OH) in the formula Na(OH) does not need a parenthesis. It can be written as NaOH.

A parenthesis is always needed when a subscript follows a radical. Take this formula for example—$Ca(OH)_2$. The small 2 after the OH is a **subscript**. It means that one molecule of this compound has two hydroxyl (OH) radicals.

How do you find the formula for a simple compound that has one or eve two radicals? It's simple. Just criss-cross the oxidation numbers—just as you did last lesson.

Here are two examples.

1. $CA^2 + (CO_3)^{-2}$

   $Ca_2(CO_3)_2$ (cancel out the 2's)

The final formula is $Ca(CO_3)$ or $CaCO_3$. Either one may be used. The name for this compound is calcium carbonate.

2. $(NH_4)^{+1} + (PO_4)^{-3}$

   $(NH_4)_3(PO_4)_1$ (cancel out the 1)

The final formula is $(NH_4)_3PO_4$. The name for this compound is ammonium phosphate.

Radical	Formula and Oxidation Number		Radical	Formula and Oxidation Number
Ammonium	$(NH_4)^{+1}$		Carbonate	$(CO_3)^{-2}$
Bicarbonate	$(HCO_3)^{-1}$		Sulfite	$(SO_3)^{-2}$
Hydroxyl	$(OH)^{-1}$		Sulfate	$(SO_4)^{-2}$
Nitrate	$(NO_3)^{-1}$		Phosphate	$(PO_4)^{-3}$

The chart above shows eight common polyatomic ions.

Now look at the chart below. The names of the eight radicals are listed in Column A.

Do the following:

- In Column B, write the formula of each polyatomic ion.
- In Column C, list the elements that make up each radical and the number of atoms of each element.
- In Column D, list the oxidation number of each polyatomic ion.

The first one has been completed for you.

	A	B	C	D
	Radical Name	Formula	Elements and Number of Atoms of Each	Oxidation Number
1.	Sulfate	SO_4	Sulfur—1 atom Oxygen—4 atoms	-2
2.	Bicarbonate			
3.	Nitrate			
4.	Ammonium			
5.	Phosphate			
6.	Carbonate			
7.	Hydroxyl			
8.	Sulfite			

NAMING COMPOUNDS

Eight compounds are listed in the chart below. Each one contains at least one radical. Name each compound. Choose from the list below.

Note: In a compound, the hydroxyl radical (OH) is called hydroxide.

calcium carbonate	sodium sulfate
ammonium nitrate	ammonium chloride
potassium hydroxide	silver nitrate
copper nitrate	ammonium hydroxide

	Formula	Name
1.	$Ag(NO_3)$	
2.	$K(OH)$	
3.	NH_4Cl	
4.	$Ca(CO_3)$	
5.	$Cu(NO_3)_2$	
6.	$NH_4(OH)$	
7.	$NH_4(NO_3)$	
8.	$Na_2(SO_4)$	

WRITING FORMULAS

Write the correct formulas in the chart below. Two formulas have been written for you.

Remember: The plus oxidation number goes first. Then criss-cross the oxidation numbers.

For example: $K^{+1} + (PO_4)^{-3}$

$K_3(PO_4)_1$

	$(OH)^{-1}$	$(NO_3)^{-1}$	$(PO_4)^{-3}$	$(HCO_3)^{-1}$	$(SO_4)^{-2}$
K^{+1}	1.	2.	3. $K_3(PO_4)$	4.	5.
Mg^{+2}	6.	7. $Mg(NO_3)_2$	8.	9.	10.
H^{+1}	11.	12.	13.	14.	15.

178

What is a polyvalent element?

28

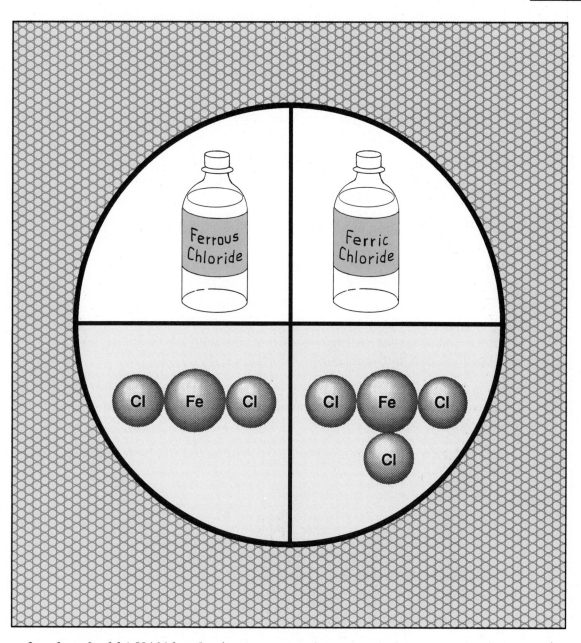

polyvalent [pahl-i-VAY-lunt]:   having more than one oxidation number

LESSON 28 | What is a polyvalent element?

All elements have an oxidation number. Many elements have more than one oxidation number. Elements with more than one oxidation number are called **polyvalent** [pahl-i-VAY-lunt]. Many elements are polyvalent. Iron (Fe), for example, has an oxidation number of +2 (Fe^{+2}). Iron can also have an oxidation number of +3 (Fe^{+3}).

A polyvalent metal can form more than one kind of compound with the same nonmetal.

For example, iron (Fe) combines with chlorine (Cl^{-1}). The compound that forms can be either $FeCl_2$ or $FeCl_3$. Which one? It depends upon the oxidation number of the iron.

If iron with an oxidation number of +2 (Fe^{+2}) takes part in the reaction we get $FeCl_2$.

$FeCl_2$ is called FERROUS chloride. The *ferr-* part comes from *ferre*, the Latin word for iron. The *-ous* ending tells us that iron with the lower oxidation number took part in the reaction.

Ferrous chloride is also called iron II chloride. The Roman numeral tells us the oxidation number of a polyvalent metal. Iron II means that the oxidation number of iron in ferrous chloride is +2.

If iron with an oxidation number of +3 (Fe^{+3}) takes part in the reaction we get $FeCl_3$.

$FeCl_3$ is called FERRIC chloride. The *-ic* ending tells us that iron with the higher oxidation number iron took part in the reaction.

Ferric chloride is also called iron III chloride. What does iron III mean?

The chart below shows five elements that are polyvalent. It shows the different oxidation numbers and the names that their compounds have.

OXIDATION NUMBERS OF METALS

Metal	Lower Oxidation Number	Name	Higher Oxidation Number	Name
Iron	Fe^{+2}	ferrous	Fe^{+3}	ferric
Mercury	Hg^{+1}	mercurous	Hg^{+2}	mercuric
Copper	Cu^{+1}	cuprous	Cu^{+2}	cupric
Gold	Au^{+1}	aurous	Au^{+3}	auric
Tin	Sn^{+2}	stannous	Sn^{+4}	stannic

1. How many oxidation numbers does each of these elements have? _____

2. The name of each lower oxidation number compound ends with _____ .
   -ous, -ic

3. The name of each higher oxidation number compounds ends with _____ .
   -ous, -ic

In a compound, "ferr-" means iron. Which elements do these stand for?

4. stann- _____   5. cupr- _____   6. aur- _____

Write the symbols and valences on the chart below. The first one has been done for you.

	Element	Symbol	Oxidation Numbers	
7.	Iron	Fe	+2	+3
8.	Tin			
9.	Gold			
10.	Mercury			
11.	Copper			

WRITING FORMULAS

Write the formula for each combination. Then answer the questions.

1. a) $Fe^{+2} + I^{-1} \longrightarrow$ | FeI_2 |

  b)   The name of this compound is _____ iodide.
  <u>ferrous, ferric</u>

2. a) $Hg^{+2} + Br^{-1} \longrightarrow$

  b)   The name of this compound is _____ bromide.
  <u>mercurous, mercuric</u>

3. a) $Sn^{+2} + F^{-1} \longrightarrow$

  b)   The name of this compound is _____ fluoride.
  <u>stannous, stannic</u>

4. a) $Cu^{+1} + S^{-2} \longrightarrow$

  b)   The name of this compound is _____ sulfide.
  <u>cuprous, cupric</u>

REACHING OUT

Which compound on this page is found in a familiar household product?

_____

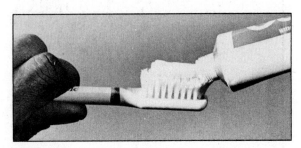

Figure A

What is formula mass?

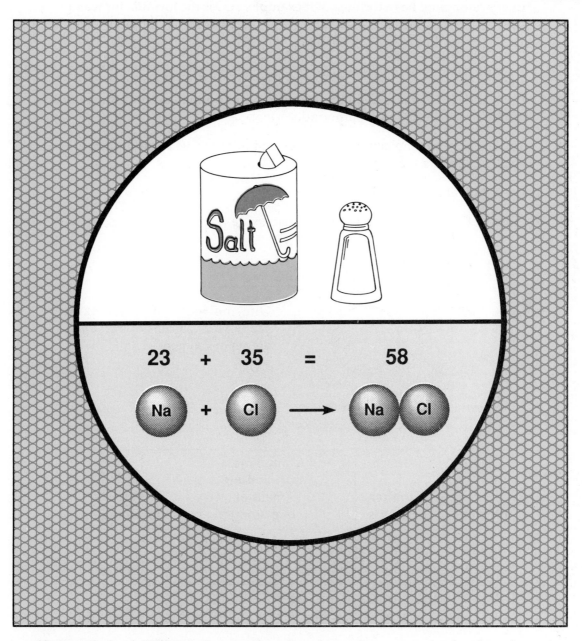

coefficient [koh-uh-FISH-unt]: number that shows how many molecules of a substance are involved in a chemical reaction

formula mass: sum of the mass numbers of all the atoms in a molecule

LESSON 29 | What is formula mass?

Every compound has a formula. For example, H_2O is the formula for water. NaCl is the formula for table salt. $C_{12}H_{22}O_{11}$ is the formula for table sugar.

Compounds are made of atoms. Atoms have mass. Therefore, compounds have mass.

If we add up the mass of all the atoms in a compound, we find the mass of one molecule of that compound.

The mass of one molecule of a compound is called its formula mass. It also is called its molecular mass.

Let's look at an example.

How to find the formula mass of ferric oxide (Fe_2O_3):

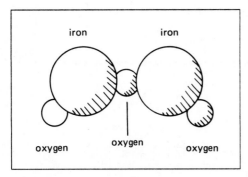

One molecule of ferric oxide (Fe_2O_3) has 2 atoms of iron and 3 atoms of oxygen.

Element	Number of atoms		Atomic mass rounded off (mass of one atom)	Total mass of atoms
Iron	2	×	56	112
Oxygen	3	×	16	48

FORMULA MASS (mass of one molecule of Fe_2O_3)   =   160

WORKING WITH FORMULA MASSES

Find the formula (molecular) mass of each compound that follows. Look up the symbol names and atomic masses. (You probably know the names of most of these symbols.)

1. Sulfuric acid H_2SO_4

Element	Number of atoms		Atomic mass	Total mass of atoms
Hydrogen	2	×		
Sulfur	1	×		
Oxygen	4	×		

Formula mass = _____

2. Sucrose (table sugar) $C_{12}H_{22}O_{11}$

Element	Number of atoms	Atomic mass	Total mass of atoms

Formula mass = _____

THE INSIDE STORY

Now let's try slightly more difficult compounds. (You will find that they are not really more difficult.) How do you handle a compound with a polyatomic ion? Molecules with polyatomic ions often have a part in parentheses and this part is followed by a subscript. $Ca(NO_3)_2$ (calcium nitrate) is a example.

Step 1 Find the number of atoms of each element.

The calcium **Ca** is <u>outside</u> the parentheses. No special figuring is needed. This formula has one atom of calcium.

The nitrate **(NO_3)_2** needs some very easy figuring. Simply multiply the number of atoms of each element within the parentheses by the subscript $(_2)$.

So we have

Number of atoms in parentheses ↘   Subscript ↙

$$N = 1 \times \boxed{2} = 2 \text{ atoms}$$
$$O = 3 \times \boxed{2} = 7 \text{ atoms}$$

Step 2 Now we can find the formula mass.

Element	Number of atoms	Atomic mass	Total mass of atoms
Calcium	1	40	40
Nitrogen	2	14	28
Oxygen	6	16	96

Formula Mass of one molecule of $Ca(NO_3)_2$ =   164

Four formulas are given. Figure out the number of atoms of each element.

1. $Fe(NO_3)_2$ Fe _____   **2.** $Al_2(SO_4)_3$ Al _____

   N _____   S _____

   O _____   O _____

Now that you know how to handle parentheses and subscripts, figure out the formula mass of each formula listed below. Find the names of the elements in the periodic table at the end of the book.

3. $Ca(OH)_2$

Element	Number of atoms	Atomic mass	Total mass of atoms
Calcium	1		
Oxygen	2		
Hydrogen	2		

Formula mass = _____

4. $Hg_2(SCN)_2$ (S, C, and N are separate elements. Naturally! Each one is a capital letter.)

Element	Number of atoms	Atomic mass	Total mass of atoms

Formula mass = _____

5. $Mg(C_7H_5O_3)_2$

Element	Number of atoms	Atomic mass	Total mass of atoms

Formula mass = _____

Sometimes you see a compound or a symbol that has a number in front of it. What does this mean?

What does the 2 mean in 2Na or NaCl? What does the 3 mean in $3H_2$?

The number in front tells you how many atoms or molecules there are. You multiply each kind of atom by this number. The number in front is called a **coefficient** [koh-uh-FISH-unt]. Let's look at some examples:

2Na	2 Na means 2 atoms of sodium
2NaCl	2NaCl means two molecules of NaCl. That means two atoms of sodium and two atoms of chlorine.
$3H_2$	Here we must multiply the **3** × 2. There are 6 atoms of hydrogen.
$3H_2O$	There are still 6 atoms of hydrogen. but we also have oxygen. **3** × 1 = 3 atoms of oxygen.

Now let's see how to handle a compound that has both parentheses and a large number.

$2Ca(NO_3)_2$	The **2** means two molecules of $Ca(NO_3)_2$.

How many atoms of each element does this mean? We must multiply the number of each kind of atom by 2.

Ca   1 × 2 = 2 atoms

N   1   ×   **2**   ×   **2**   =   4 atoms

Subscript	Coefficient

O   3   ×   **2**   ×   **2**   =   12 atoms

An important thing to remember!

A coefficient in front of an element or a compound goes only with that element or compound. A plus (+) or an arrow (→) tells us where the value of the coefficient ends. For example:

$$4Fe + 3O_2 \rightarrow 2Fe_2O_3$$

- The 4 in front of the Fe goes only with the Fe.
- The 3 in front of the O_2 goes only with the O_2.
- But the 2 in front of Fe_2O_3 goes with the Fe_2 and the O_3. They are part of the same molecule.

LET'S JUST COUNT

Count the number of atoms in each of the following:

1. $2Ba(OH)_2$ Ba _____

    O _____

    H _____

2. $4Al_2(SO_4)_3$ Al _____

    S _____

    O _____

3. $3Ba(OH_2)$ Ba _____

    O _____

    H _____

4. $2Mg(C_7H_5O_3)_2$ Mg _____

    C _____

    H _____

    O _____

NOW BACK TO MASSES

Now you know how to handle formulas that have both parentheses and numbers in front. How do we figure masses for these formulas?

Simple, you have already learned that the formula mass of $Ca(NO_3)_2$ is 164. This means that one molecule has a mass of 164.

What is the mass of $2Ca(NO_3)_2$? Easy! Just multiply the formula mass by 2.

Mass of $2Ca(NO_3)_2$: $2 \times 164 =$ 328   =   FORMULA MASS

The formula mass of $Ba(OH)_2$ is 171. Figure the mass of each of the following:

1. $2Ba(OH)_2$ _____

2. $3Ba(OH)_2$ _____

The formula mass of $Pb(NO_3)_2$ is 331. Figure the mass of each of the following:

3. $2Pb(NO_3)_2$ _____

4. $4PB(NO_3)_2$ _____

REACHING OUT

1. Find the formula mass of this compound: $Fe(NH_4)_2 (SO_4)_2$.

_____

2. Find the mass of the following: $2Al_2(SO_3)_3$

_____

What is a chemical equation?

30

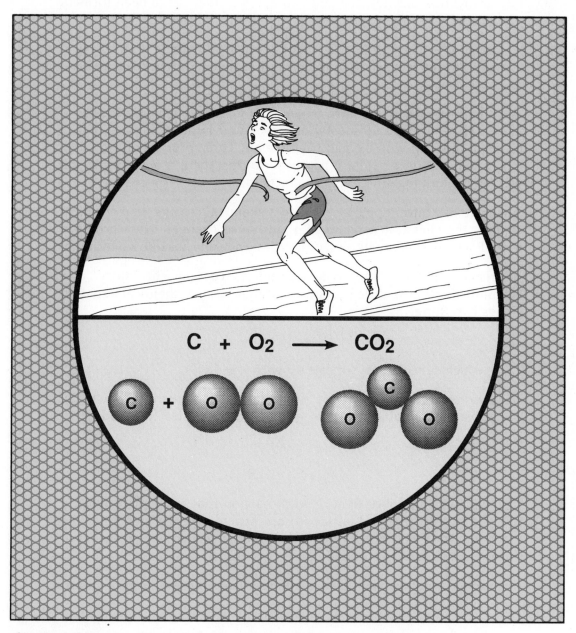

$$C + O_2 \longrightarrow CO_2$$

chemical change: change in matter that produces new products
chemical equation: set of symbols and formulas that describe a chemical change
physical change: change in matter that does not produce any new products
product: a substance that is produced in a chemical reaction (change)
reactant: substance that takes part in a chemical reaction (change)

LESSON 30 | What is a chemical equation?

You may tear a sheet of paper into tiny pieces, but you still have paper. Each piece is still paper no matter how small. The way the atoms are linked together has not changed. No new products have been formed. The properties of the paper have not changed. Neither has its formula.

A change like tearing paper is called a **physical change**. In a physical change, only the appearance of a substance changes. The chemical makeup does not change.

What happens when you burn paper? You no longer have paper. Paper is a compound made up mostly of carbon and hydrogen. When paper burns, it links up with oxygen from the air. Three products form—ash, water, and carbon dioxide. When paper burns, there is a change in the way atoms link together. New products form. Properties change.

A change like burning paper is called a **chemical change**. In a chemical change, the chemical makeup of a substance changes. New products form. Each product has its own properties. Each one has its own formula.

A chemical change is caused by a chemical reaction. The "story" of a chemical reaction is called a **chemical equation**. A chemical equation shows two things:

- which substance(s) we start out with

- which substance(s) we end up with

The substance or substances we <u>start out with</u> are called the **reactants**. The substance or substances we <u>end up with</u> are called the **products**.

This is an example of a chemical equation:

$$Fe + S \rightarrow FeS$$

This equation describes the chemical reaction that takes place when a mixture of iron (Fe) and sulfur (S) are heated. The Fe and S are the reactants. The FeS (iron sulfide) is the product. The arrow means "produces" or "yields."

The properties of iron sulfide are different from those of iron or sulfur.

Figure A *Sodium chloride (NaCl)*

Table salt (NaCl) is also called sodium chloride. It is a white solid. Your body contains this salt. It is necessary for life.

Figure B *Sodium (Na)*

Sodium (Na) is a very dangerous solid. It can explode in water.

Swallowing sodium can cause death.

Figure C *Chlorine (Cl)*

Chlorine (Cl) is a deadly greenish-yellow gas. If you inhale enough of this gas, it could be fatal.

Table salt can be melted. If an electric current passes through melted sodium chloride, a chemical reaction takes place. This is the chemical equation for this reaction.

$$2NaCl \rightarrow 2Na + Cl_2$$

Answer these questions.

1. This reaction has one reactant. Name that reactant. _____

2. The reactant in its natural state is a _____ .

solid, liquid, gas

3. The reactant _____ dangerous.

is, is not

4. Name the products. _____   _____

5. What is the state of sodium? _____

6. Is sodium dangerous? _____

7. Are the properties of sodium the same as the properties of sodium chloride?

   _____

8. What is the state of chlorine? _____

9. Is chlorine dangerous? _____

10. Are the properties of chlorine the same as the properties of sodium chloride?

    _____

11. In a chemical reaction, properties _____ change.

do, do not

12. Name the kinds of atoms on the reactant side of this equation. _____

13. Name the kinds of atoms on the product side. _____   _____

14. The kinds of atoms on the reactant side _____ the same as the atoms
    on the resultant side.

are, are not

15. Are they in the same form? _____

16. The atoms in the reactant are part of _____ .

a compound, two elements

17. The atoms in the product are part of _____ .

a compound, two elements

18. The arrangements of the atoms _____ changed.

has, has not

19. In this reaction, atoms have _____ .

separated, linked up

20. In a chemical reaction, the arrangement of the elements _____ change.

does, does not

192

PRODUCT OR REACTANT?

Five chemical equations are given below. Below each equation you will find the name of each substance in this equation. For each chemical equation:

- Write reactant next to each substance that is a reactant.

- Write product next to each substance that is a product.

1. **Zn + FeSO4 → ZnSO4 + Fe**

   Zinc sulfate _____   Iron _____

   Zinc _____   Iron sulfate _____

2. **4HCl + MnO$_2$ → MnCl2 + 2H$_2$O + Cl$_2$**

   Chlorine _____

   Manganese chloride _____

   Manganese dioxide _____

   Water _____

   Hydrochloric acid (Hydrogen chloride) _____

3. **H$_2$SO$_4$ + BaCl$_2$ → 2HCl + BaSO$_4$**

   Barium chloride _____

   Hydrochloric acid (hydrogen chloride) _____

   Barium sulfate _____

   Sulfuric acid (hydrogen sulfate) _____

4. **Br$_2$ + 2KI → 2KBr + I$_2$**

   Potassium bromide _____   Iodine _____

   Bromine _____   Potassium iodide _____

5. **2ZnS + 3O$_2$ → 2ZnO + 2SO$_2$**

   Oxygen _____   Sulfur dioxide _____

   Zinc oxide _____   Zinc sulfide _____

Complete each statement using a term or terms from the list below. Write your answers in the spaces provided. Some words may be used more than once.

products	right	physical
chemical equation	take part	yields
new	chemical	reaction
arrow	reactants	left

1. A change in which no new products are formed is called a ———————— change.

2. A change in which new products are formed is called a ———————— change.

3. Another way of saying "chemical change" is "chemical ————————."

4. A set of symbols and formulas that describes a chemical reaction is called a

   ————————————.

5. A chemical equation tells which substances ———————— in a chemical

   reaction. It also tells which ———————— substances are formed.

6. The substances that take part in a chemical reaction are called the

   ————————.

7. The new substances that form in a chemical reaction are called the

   ————————.

8. In a chemical equation, the reactants are on the ———————— side. The

   products are on the ———————— side.

9. In a chemical reaction, the reactants and products are separated by an

   ———————— .

10. The arrow means "produces" or "————————".

REACHING OUT

Sodium hydroxide reacts with hydrochloric acid (hydrogen chloride) to produce sodium chloride (table salt) and water. Write the equation that shows this reaction.

————————————————————————————————————

Does a chemical reaction destroy matter?

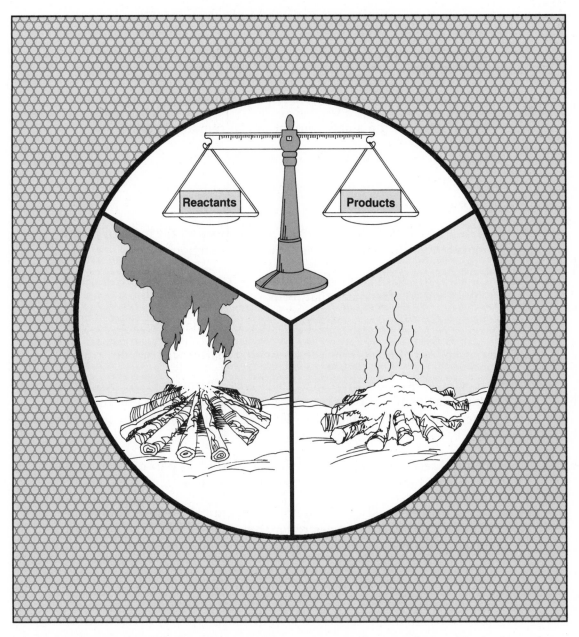

31

Law of Conservation of Matter: scientific statement that says that a chemical reaction does not destroy or create matter.

LESSON 31 | Does a chemical reaction destroy matter?

In a chemical reaction, atoms change the way they are linked together. New products form. But are any atoms lost during the changeover? Is any matter destroyed?

The burning of wood and rusting are two examples of chemical reactions.

- Wood burns, and a small amount of ash remains behind.

- A car rusts, and it looks like it's wearing away.

It surely seems that some matter is lost. But is it really? This is how we can find out:

1. Find the mass of the reactants. That means find the mass of <u>all</u> the substances that take part in a chemical reaction.

2. Then find the mass of the products. That means find the mass of <u>all</u> the new substances that form.

If there is a loss of mass, then we know that some matter was destroyed.

If there is no loss of mass, then we know that matter was not destroyed.

In any chemical reaction, there is no mass loss. The mass of the products is the same as the mass of the reactants. In other words, we end up with the same mass as we started with. This means that no matter was destroyed.

In a chemical reaction, matter is not destroyed. This is part of a scientific statement called the **Law of Conservation of Matter**.

Can matter be destroyed? Yes! But not in a chemical reaction. It takes an atomic or nuclear reaction to destroy matter. When matter is destroyed, it changes into energy. This is the idea behind atomic energy.

Look at Figures A and B. Then answer the questions.

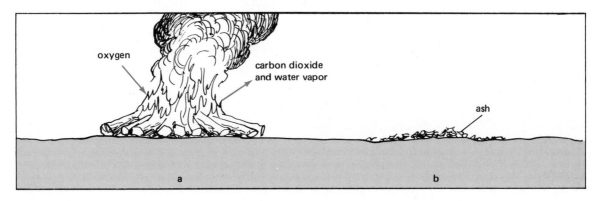

Figure A

Wood, like paper, is made up mostly of carbon and hydrogen.

When wood burns, it links up with oxygen. The reaction produces ash, carbon dioxide, and water vapor. (Heat energy is also produced. But energy has no weight.)

Wood + Oxygen → Ash + Carbon dioxide + Water vapor

1. Name the reactants when wood burns. _____

2. Name the products. _____

3. Where does the oxygen come from? _____

4. The ash remains behind. What happens to the carbon dioxide and water?_____

   _____

5. If the reactants have a mass of 10 kilograms, what will the mass of the products be?

   _____

6. Is any matter lost?_____

7. Is matter lost during any chemical reaction? _____

8. In a chemical reaction, the mass of the products equals the mass of the

   _____ . In other words, "the mass you start with is the mass you

   _____ ."

9. Name the scientific statement that tells us that matter is not destroyed during a

   chemical reaction. _____

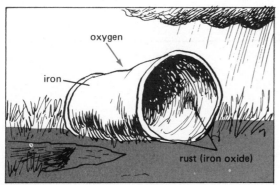

When iron rusts, it links up with oxygen. This is the formula for the reaction:

$$4Fe + 3O_2 \rightarrow 2Fe_2O_3$$

Iron   Oxygen   Iron oxide
(Rust)

Figure B

1. Name the reactants. _____   _____

2. Where did the oxygen come from? _____

3. What is the chemical name of the product? _____

4. What is the common name of the product? _____

Look at the equation. Answer the questions.

5. How many atoms of iron did we start with? _____

6. The atomic mass of iron is 56. What is the mass of all the iron atoms? _____

7. How many atoms of oxygen did we start with? _____

8. The atomic mass of oxygen is 16. What is the mass of all the oxygen atoms?

_____

9. Altogether, what is the mass of the reactants? _____

10. How many atoms of iron did we end with? _____

11. What is the mass of all these atoms? _____

12. How many atoms of oxygen did we end with? _____

13. What is the mass of all these atoms? _____

14. Altogether, what is the mass of the product? _____

15. Is the mass of the product the same as the mass of the reactants? _____

16. Was any matter lost? _____

17. How do you know? _____

18. Is any matter destroyed in a chemical reaction? _____

19. What happens to atoms during a chemical reaction? _____

_____

20. The equation for rusting is a "balanced" equation. What do you think this means?

_____

_____

COUNTING ATOMS

Let's work with the equation in a different way. This time let's just count atoms.

$$4Fe + 3O_2 \rightarrow 2Fe_2O_3$$

1. Name the kinds of atoms of the reactant side of the equation. _____

_____

2. Name the kinds of atoms on the product side. _____ _____

3. The kinds of atom on the product side _____ the same as the
   kinds of atoms on the reactant side.   are, are not

4. How many atoms of iron are there on the reactant side? _____

5. How many atoms of iron are there on the product side? _____

6. How many atoms of oxygen are there on the reactant side? _____

7. How many atoms of oxygen are there on the product side? _____

8,. The number of any kind of atom _____ the same on both sides of
    the equation.   is, is not

9. If the number of each kind of atom is the same on both sides of the equation,

   then what else is equal? _____

10. This shows that matter _____ destroyed.
                           was, was not

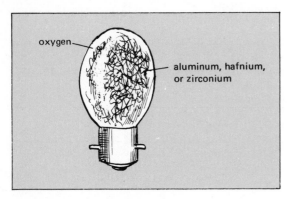

Figure C *Fresh flashbulb*

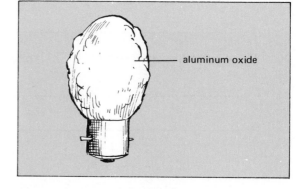

Figure D *Used flashbulb*

What You Need to Know (Background Information)

Everyone knows what a flashbulb is. It gives off a bright flash of light. It lets us take pictures where there is little light.

A flashbulb contains oxygen and shreds of metal like aluminum, hafnium, or zirconium.

When a bulb "goes off," a chemical reaction takes place. The oxygen links up with the metal. This produces an oxide of the metal. For example, if the bulb contains aluminum, aluminum oxide forms.

This is the equation for the reaction:

$$4AL + 3O_2 \rightarrow 2Al_2O_3 \; (+ \text{Light} + \text{Heat})$$

What You Need (Materials)

balance scale   heat proof pad
6 volt battery   two insulated wires
fireproof cloth   a flashbulb

What To Do (Procedure)

1. Find the mass of the bulb before you flash it. What is the mass of the bulb?

   _____ grams

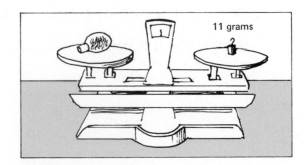

Figure E

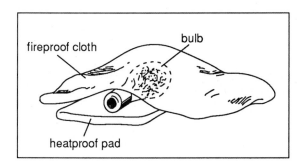

Figure F

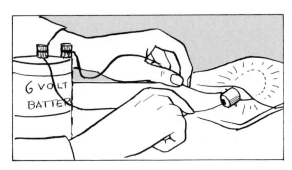

Figure G

Figure H

2. Place the bulb on the heat proof pad. Cover most of the bulb with the fireproof cloth. Keep only the end of the metal base uncovered. (Figure F)

3. Flash the bulb. (Figure G)

4. Uncover the bulb. Wait about one minute until it cools. Then weigh it again. (Figure H)

What is the mass of the bulb now?

_____ grams

What You Learned (Observations)

1. What was the mass of the bulb before it was flashed? _____

2. What was the mass of the bulb after it was flashed? _____

3. A flashbulb "going off" causes a

_____ change.
physical, chemical

4. If a chemical reaction destroys matter, than the bulb would become

_____ .
heavier, lighter

5. Did the bulb become lighter after it was flashed? _____

Something To Think About (Conclusions)

1. Matter _____ destroyed.
was, was not

2. A chemical reaction _____ destroy matter.
does, does not

BALANCED OR NOT BALANCED?

Four equations are listed below. Two are balanced. Two are not. Figure out which ones are balanced. (Hint: Counting atoms is the easiest way.)

Equations

A. $An + H_2SO_4 \rightarrow ZnSO_4 + H_2$

B. $Mg + O_2 \rightarrow 2MgO$

C. $Na_2S + 2HCl \rightarrow 2NaCl + H_2S$

D. $H_2S + SO_2 \rightarrow 3S + 2H_2O$

1. Which equations are balanced? _____

2. Which equations are not balanced? _____

3. Which equations show the Law of Conservation of Matter? _____

4. Which equations do not show the Law of Conservation of Matter? _____

5. Which equations are not possible? _____

REACHING OUT

Figure I *Uranium fuel*

A nuclear reaction destroys matter. Nuclear fuel, like uranium, changes to energy.

How can we show that matter is lost in a nuclear reaction? (Hint: Look back at the flashbulb experiment.)

_____

_____

_____

_____

_____

_____

What is a synthesis reaction?

32

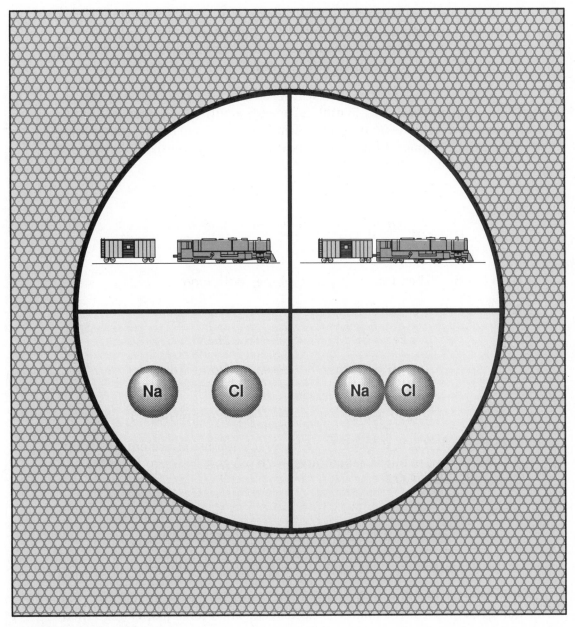

synthesis [SIN-thuh-sis] **reaction:** combining of several substances to form a more complicated substance

LESSON 32 | What is a synthesis reaction?

Chemical reactions are happening around you all the time. A match burns. A car rusts. food spoils. Leaves decay. These are just a few chemical reactions.

Probably the most important chemical reactions take place in your body. They are happening this very moment. Digestion is a chemical process. So is respiration. In every one of your trillions of cells, chemical reactions are taking place all the time. Life depends upon chemical reactions.

There are several kinds of chemical reactions. One kind is the **synthesis** [SIN-thuh-sis] **reaction**. "Synthesis" means a putting together. A synthesis reaction combines substances, usually elements, to form a compound. When the compound forms, we say it has been synthesized. Below is a "model" of a synthesis reaction.

$$A + B \longrightarrow AB$$

$$\text{Element} + \text{Element} \longrightarrow \text{Compound}$$

Let's study two synthesis reactions.

RUSTING   When iron rusts, it <u>combines</u> with oxygen.

Remember this equation?

$$4Fe + 3O_2 \longrightarrow 2Fe_2O_3$$

Iron + Oxygen $\longrightarrow$ Iron oxide (rust)

Element + Element $\xrightarrow[\text{to form}]{\text{link up}}$ Compound

THE BURNING OF CARBON   Charcoal is made of the element carbon (C). When carbon burns, it <u>combines</u> with oxygen. This produces the gas carbon dioxide (CO_2).

$$C + O_2 \longrightarrow CO_2$$

Carbon + Oxygen $\xrightarrow[\text{to form}]{\text{link up}}$ Carbon dioxide

Element + Element $\longrightarrow$ Compound

A synthesis reaction is like any other kind of chemical reaction. No matter is created. No matter is destroyed. The atoms just change their arrangement.

Look at Figures A through E and read the explanation. Then answer the questions with each.

When hydrogen explodes, it combines with oxygen. Water is produced. This equation shows what happens:

$$H_2 + O_2 \longrightarrow H_2O$$
Hydrogen + Oxygen $\longrightarrow$ Water

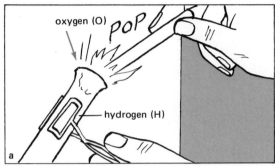

Figure A

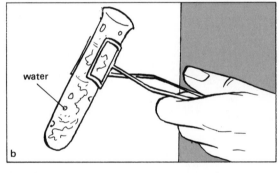

Figure B

1. Hydrogen is_____ .
   <u>an element, a compound</u>

2. Oxygen is _____.
   <u>an element, a compound</u>

3. Water is _____ .
   <u>an element, a compound</u>

4. Is the formation of water a synthesis reaction? _____

5. Why is the formation of water a synthesis reaction? _____

   _____

   _____

When powdered sulfur and iron filings are heated together, they form iron sulfide.

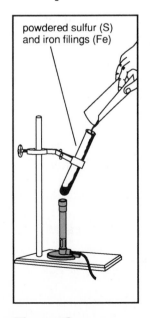

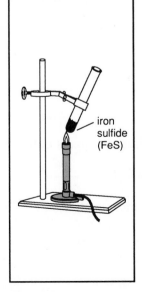

This equation shows what happens:

$$Fe + S \longrightarrow FeS$$
Iron + Sulfur $\longrightarrow$ Iron sulfide

1. Iron is _____ .
   <u>an element, a compound</u>

2. Sulfur is _____ .
   <u>an element, a compound</u>

3. Iron sulfide is _____ .
   <u>an element, a compound</u>

4. What happens to the iron and sulfur when they form iron sulfide? _____

   _____

Figure C　　　　**Figure D**

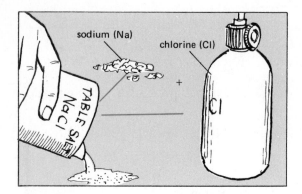

Sodium combines with chlorine to form sodium chloride—common table salt.

This equation shows what happens:

$$Na \quad + \quad Cl \quad \longrightarrow \quad NaCl$$

Sodium + Chlorine ⟶ Sodium chloride

Figure E

1. Sodium is _____ .
   _{an element, a compound}

2. Chlorine is _____ .
   _{an element, a compound}

3. Sodium chloride is _____ .
   _{an element, a compound}

4. What kind of reaction is the formation of sodium chloride? _____

   Why? _____

YOUR OWN WORDS, PLEASE

1. What does "synthesis" mean? _____

   _____

2. What does "synthesis reaction" mean? _____

   _____

Two synthesis equations are shown below. They are different from the ones you have already seen.

Equation I $CO_2 + C \quad \longrightarrow \quad 2CO_2$

Equation II $CO_2 + H_2O \quad \longrightarrow \quad H_2CO_3$

3. How is Equation I different from the other synthesis equations in this lesson?

   _____

4. How is Equation II different from the other synthesis equations in this lesson?

   _____

IDENTIFYING SYNTHESIS REACTIONS

Ten equations are listed below. Some are synthesis reactions. Some are not. Make a check (✓) in the correct box next to each equation.

	Equation	A Synthesis Reaction	Not a Synthesis Reaction
1.	$2K + Br_2 \longrightarrow 2KBr$		
2.	$2H_2O \longrightarrow 2H_2 + O_2$		
3.	$NaCl \longrightarrow Na + Cl$		
4.	$4Au + 3O_2 \longrightarrow 2Au_2O_3$		
5.	$2Na + 2HCl \longrightarrow 2NaCl + H_2$		
6.	$Cu + Br_2 \longrightarrow CuBr_2$		
7.	$Zn + S \longrightarrow ZnS$		
8.	$2NA + Br_2 \longrightarrow 2NaBr$		
9.	$2HgO \longrightarrow 2Hg + O_2$		
10.	$2Na + I_2 \longrightarrow 2NaI$		

TRUE OR FALSE

In the space provided, write "true" if the sentence is true. Write "false" if the sentence is false.

_____ 1. There is only one kind of chemical reaction.

_____ 2. A synthesis reaction separates a compound into its elements.

_____ 3. The reactants of every synthesis reaction are elements.

_____ 4. The product of a synthesis reaction is a compound.

_____ 5. Chemical reactions take place only in the laboratory.

WORD SEARCH

The list on the left contains words that you have used in this Lesson. Find and circle each word where it appears. in the box. the spellings may go in any direction: up, down, left, right, or diagonally.

MATTER

POLYVALENT

RADICAL

MASS

REACTANT

FORMULA

PHYSICAL

PRODUCT

YIELDS

CHEMICAL

C	T	L	A	C	I	S	Y	H	P	A
H	O	N	L	A	C	I	M	E	H	C
I	Y	I	E	L	D	S	C	N	O	D
M	M	C	A	L	U	M	R	O	F	M
T	N	A	T	C	A	E	R	T	T	Y
N	E	L	S	H	W	V	H	G	C	L
R	I	A	L	S	S	A	Y	L	U	L
A	L	R	A	D	I	C	A	L	D	I
I	S	Y	R	A	G	L	E	Y	O	M
J	E	R	R	R	H	D	W	I	R	P
C	L	R	E	T	T	A	M	E	P	I

REACHING OUT

Most compounds made of only two elements have names ending in *-ide*. For example:

NaCl = sodium chloride

K_2S = potassium sulfide

Can you name these compounds?

	Formula	Name
1.	CaO	
2.	KI	
3.	NaBr	
4.	AgF	
5.	MgCl	

What is a decomposition reaction?

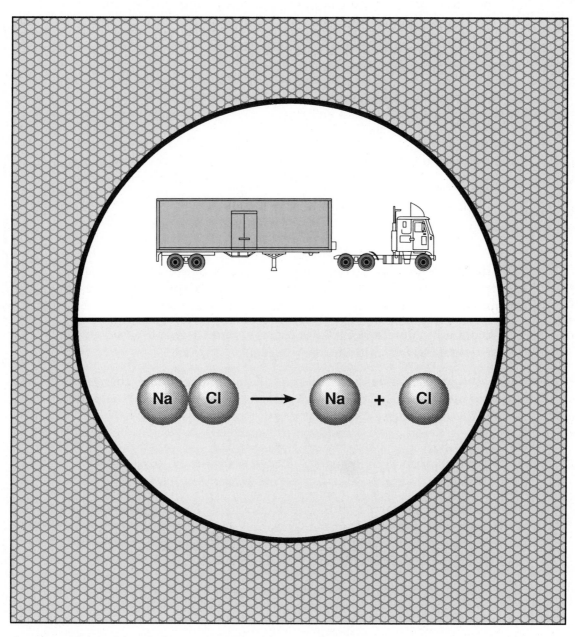

decomposition [dee-kahm-puh-ZISH-un]: breakdown of a substance into simpler substances

electrolysis [i-lek-TRAHL-uh-sis]: decomposition of a substance by means of electricity

LESSON 33 | What is a decomposition reaction?

Synthesis reactions build compounds. Anything that can be built can also be taken apart. The breakdown of a compound into simpler substances is called **decomposition** [dee-kahn-puh-ZISH-un]. Decomposition is a chemical process.

Let us look at two examples.

1. Common table salt (sodium chloride) is a compound. It is composed of the elements sodium and chlorine.

Sodium chloride can be melted. If electricity is passed through melted sodium chloride, it decomposes. The molecules unlock. They change back to atoms of sodium and chlorine. This equation shows the reaction:

$$2NaCl \xrightarrow[\text{into}]{\text{breaks down}} 2Na \quad + \quad Cl_2$$

Sodium chloride		Sodium	Chlorine
(compound)		(element)	(element)

The decomposition of a compound by means of electricity is called **electrolysis** [i-lek-TRAHL-uh-sis]. Only certain compounds can be decomposed by electrolysis. Usually these compounds are liquids.

2. Potassium chlorate (KClO3) is a compound. It is composed of the elements potassium, chlorine, and oxygen.

Heat decomposes potassium chlorate. Potassium chlorate changes to oxygen and potassium chloride (a simpler compound). This equation shows the reaction:

$$2KClO_3 \longrightarrow 2KCl \quad + \quad 3O_2$$

Potassium chlorate		Potassium Chloride	Oxygen
(compound)		(a simpler compound)	(element)

Notice that the decomposition is not complete. The oxygen has been separated. But the potassium and chlorine are still joined to form the compound potassium chloride. Another kind of decomposition reaction can separate potassium chloride into its elements.

Only certain compounds are decomposed with heat.

Look at Figure A. Then answer the questions or fill in the blanks.

Electrolysis decomposes water. This is the equation for the reaction:

$$2H_2O \longrightarrow 2H_2 + O_2$$

Water — Hydrogen + Oxygen

1. What is the formula for water? _____

2. Water is _____.
   (an element, a compound)

3. Name the elements that make up water.

   _____

4. Name the process that decomposes water.

   _____

5. What kind of energy is used?

   _____

6. When water decomposes. It changes to the

   elements _____ and

   _____ .

7. Water is in the _____ state.
   (solid, liquid, gas)

8. Hydrogen is in the _____ state.
   (solid, liquid, gas)

9. Oxygen is in the _____ state.
   (solid, liquid, gas)

10. Which is simpler, water or the elements that make up water? _____

    _____

11. Decomposition _____ compounds.
    (builds up, breaks down)

12. Can electrolysis decompose every compound? _____

13. Name another compound that can be decomposed with electrolysis.

    _____

14. A compound that can be separated by electrolysis must be in which state of matter?

    _____

Figure A

211

Look at Figure B. Answer the questions.

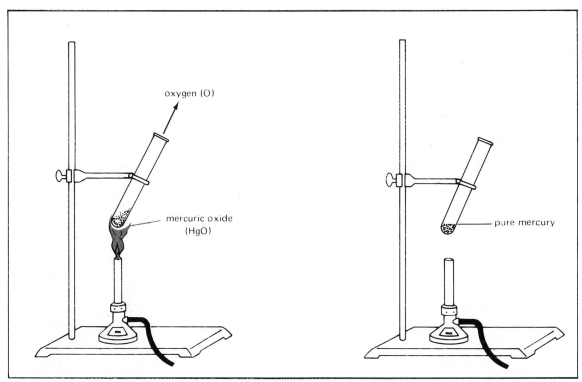

Figure B

Mercuric oxide is a solid. Heat decomposes mercuric oxide. This is the equation for the reaction.

$$2HgO \xrightarrow{\text{heat}} 2Hg + O_2$$

Mercuric oxide   Mercury   +   Oxygen

1. What is the formula for mercuric oxide? _____

2. Mercuric oxide is _____ .

                             an element, a compound

3. Name the elements that make up mercuric oxide. _____

_____

4. What happens when mercuric oxide is heated? _____

5. What kind of energy decomposes mercuric oxide? _____

6. When mercuric oxide decomposes, it changes to the elements_____ and

_____ .

7. Mercuric oxide is in the _____ state.

                         solid, liquid, gas

8. Mercury is in the _____ state.
solid, liquid, gas

9. Oxygen is in the _____ state.
solid, liquid, gas

10. Which is simpler: mercuric oxide or the elements that make up mercuric oxide?

_____

11. The mercury _____.
stays in the test tube, escapes into the air

12. The oxygen _____.
stays in the test tube, escapes into the air

13. Can heat decompose every compound? _____

14. Name another compound that can be decomposed by heat. _____

FILL IN THE BLANK

Complete each statement using a term or terms from the list below. Write your answers in the spaces provided.

heating	mercuric oxide	electrolysis
Potassium chlorate	synthesis	molten sodium chloride
liquid	fewer	decomposition
simpler	water	

1. The combining of substances to form a compound is called _____.

2. The breakdown of a compound into simpler substances is called

_____ .

3. Two methods used to decompose compounds are _____ and

_____ .

4. For a compound to decompose by electrolysis, it must be in a _____ state.

5. Two compounds that can be decomposed by electrolysis are

_____ and _____ .

6. Two compounds that can be decomposed by heat are _____

and _____ .

7. Atoms are _____ than molecules.

8. KCl is a simpler compound than $KClO_3$ because KCl has _____ elements and atoms.

MATCHING

Match each term in Column A with its description in Column B. Write the correct letter in the space provided.

Column A

_____ 1. synthesis reaction

_____ 2. decomposition reaction

_____ 3. electrolysis and heat

_____ 4. electrolysis

_____ 5. an element

Column B

a) breaks down compounds

b) uses electricity

c) methods of decomposition

d) simpler than a compound

e) builds compounds

IDENTIFYING DECOMPOSITION REACTIONS

Ten chemical equations are listed below. Some are decomposition reactions. Some are not. Mark a (✓) in the correct box next to each equation.

	Equation	Decomposition Reaction	Not a Decomposition Reaction
1.	$CuCl_2 \rightarrow Cu + Cl_2$		
2.	$3Hf + 2N_2 \rightarrow Hf_3N_4$		
3.	$Zn + 2HCl \rightarrow ZnCl_2 + H_2$		
4.	$H_2CO_3 \rightarrow H_2O + CO_2$		
5.	$2NaOH \rightarrow 2Na + O_2 + H_2$		
6.	$Fe + S \rightarrow FeS$		
7.	$CaCO_3 \rightarrow CaO + CO_2$		
8.	$4P + 5O_2 \rightarrow 2P_2O_5$		
9.	$C + O_2 \rightarrow CO_2$		
10.	$Ca(OH)_2 \rightarrow CaO + H_2O$		

REACHING OUT

1. Does boiling decompose water? _____

2. What does boiling do to water? _____

_____

What is a replacement reaction?

34

replacement: reaction in which one kind of matter replaces another kind

LESSON 34 | What is a replacement reaction?

Imagine that three children are playing.

Two are holding hands. The other is alone.

The child that was alone now joins the others. He takes the place of one of the children.

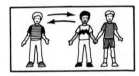

Now a different child is alone.

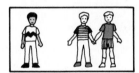

We have the same children that we started with. But, now they are arranged in a different way.

Some chemical reactions work like this. A free element takes the place of or replaces another element of a compound.

The element that was replaced is now "free."

$$A \quad + \quad BC \quad \longrightarrow \quad AC \quad + \quad B$$

free element   compound   new compound   new free element

Let's study an actual replacement reaction—one between zinc (Zn) and hydrochloric acid (HCl).

The zinc is the "free" element. The hydrochloric acid is in the compound.

$$Zn \quad + \quad 2HCl \quad \longrightarrow \quad ZnCl_2 \quad + \quad H_2$$

The zinc replaces the hydrogen.   The hydrogen is set free.

The reaction produces a new compound, zinc chloride ($ZnCl_2$), and free hydrogen (H_2). Notice that the elements we started with are the elements we ended with. They are just arranged in a different way.

This kind of reaction is called a single replacement reaction. In a single replacement reaction, a free element replaces a different element of a compound.

216

UNDERSTANDING SINGLE REPLACEMENT REACTIONS

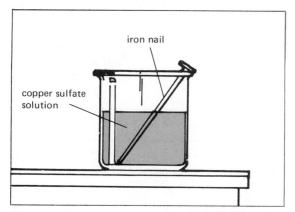

Figure A

Figure B

What You Need (Materials)

iron nail
copper sulfate solution
beaker

How To Do The Experiment (Procedure)

Place an iron nail in copper sulfate solution.

Remove the nail in a few minutes.

What You Saw (Observations)

The nail is coated with copper.

This is the equation for the reaction.

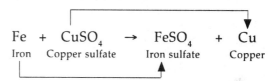

$$Fe + CuSO_4 \rightarrow FeSO_4 + Cu$$

Iron   Copper sulfate   Iron sulfate   Copper

1. Name the free element we started with. _____

2. Name the compound we started with. _____

3. Name the free element we ended with. _____

4. Name the compound we ended with. _____

5. **a)** Which element did the iron replace? _____

   b) What happened to this element? _____

6. What do we call this kind of chemical reaction? _____

7. What happens during a single replacement reaction? _____

_____

IDENTIFYING SINGLE REPLACEMENT REACTIONS

Six equations are listed below. Some are single replacement reactions. Some are not. Mark a check (✓) in the correct box next to each equation.

	Equation	Single replacement reaction	Not a single replacement reaction
1.	$C + 2S \rightarrow CS_2$		
2.	$H_2O_2 \rightarrow H_2 + O_2$		
3.	$2Al + 6HCl \rightarrow 2AlCl_3 + 3H_2$		
4.	$2K + Cl_2 \rightarrow 2KCl$		
5.	$Zn + PbO \rightarrow ZnO + Pb$		
6.	$Fe + CuSO_4 \rightarrow FeSO_4 + Cu$		

DOUBLE REPLACEMENT REACTIONS

A <u>single</u> replacement reaction takes place between an element and a compound. The free element replaces one of the elements of the compound. This produces a new compound and a new free element.

$$A \quad + \quad BC \quad \rightarrow \quad AC \quad + \quad B$$
free element compound   new compound new free element

A <u>double</u> replacement reaction takes place between <u>two</u> compounds. A part of one compound changes place with a part of the other compound.

Let us use playing children as models again to see what happens.

Children A and B stand for compound AB.
Children C and D stand for compound CD.

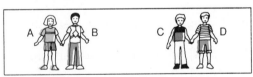

Figure C

Child A changes place with child C.

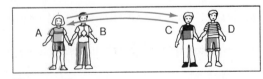

Figure D

What do we have now? Instead of compounds AB and CD, we have two new compounds— CB and AD.

When there are two changeovers, a double replacement has taken place.

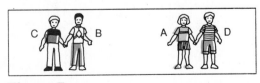

Figure E

New let us study an actual double replacement reaction—the reaction between sodium hydroxide (NaOH), and hydrochloric acid (HCl).

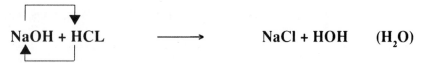

NaOH + HCL $\longrightarrow$ NaCl + HOH   (H₂O)

- The sodium and hydrogen change places.
- Two new compounds form—NaCl (common table salt) and HOH (water).

Now you try. Read each equation carefully. Then answer the questions or fill in the blanks with each.

Equation I   BaCl₂   +   Na₂SO₄   →   BaSO₄   +   2NaCl
                  Barium chloride   Sodium sulfate   Barium sulfate   Sodium chloride

1. Name the reactants. _____ _____

2. The reactants are _____ .
                  both elements, both compounds, an element and a compound

3. The barium changed places with the _____ .
                  sulfate, chlorine, sodium

4. Name the products. _____ _____

5. The products are _____ .
                  both elements, both compounds, an element and a compound

6. What kind of chemical reaction is this? _____

7. Double replacement is the reaction of two _____ to form two new

   _____ .

Equation II   AgNO₃   +   NaBr   →   AgBr   +   NaNO₃
                  Silver nitrate   Sodium bromide   Silver bromide   Sodium nitrate

8. Name the reactants. _____ _____

9. The reactants are _____ .
                  both elements, both compounds, an element and a compound

10. The silver changed places with the _____ .
                  sodium, bromine, nitrate

11. Name the products. _____ _____

12. The products are _____ .
                  both elements, both compounds, an element and a compound

13. What kind of chemical reaction is this? _____

IDENTIFYING DOUBLE REPLACEMENT REACTIONS

Eight equations are listed below. Some are double replacement reactions. Some are not. Mark a check (✓) in the correct box next to each equation.

	Equation	Double replacement reaction	Not a double replacement reaction
1.	$Mg(OH_2) + 2HCl \rightarrow MgCl_2 + 2HOH$		
2.	$C_6H_{10}O_5 + H_2O \rightarrow C_6H_{12}O_6$		
3.	$Na_2SO_4 + BaCl_2 \rightarrow 2NaCl + BaSO_4$		
4.	$3Mg + N_2 \rightarrow Mg_3N_2$		
5.	$H_2SO_4 + BaCl_2 \rightarrow 2HCl + BaSO_4$		
6.	$ZnCO_3 \rightarrow ZnO + CO_2$		
7.	$CuSO_4 + H_2S \rightarrow H_2SO_4 + CuS$		
8.	$NH_4NO_3 \rightarrow 2H_2O + N_2O$		

IDENTIFYING CHEMICAL REACTIONS

Ten chemical equations are listed below. Identify each kind of reaction: synthesis, decomposition, single replacement, or double replacement.

	Equation	Kind of reaction
1.	$N_2 + 3H_2 \rightarrow 2NH_3$	
2.	$2Br_2 + 2H_2O \rightarrow 4HBr + O_2$	
3.	$Mg + 2HCl \rightarrow MgCl_2 + H_2$	
4.	$2KBr + H_2SO_4 \rightarrow K_2SO_4 + 2HBr$	
5.	$H_2SO_3 \rightarrow H_2O + SO_2$	
6.	$Na_2S + 2HCl \rightarrow 2NaCl + H_2S$	
7.	$2Na + I_2 \rightarrow 2NaI$	
8.	$NaCl + AgNO_3 \rightarrow NaNO_3 + AgCl$	
9.	$H_2 + Cl_2 \rightarrow 2HCl$	
10.	$H_2CO_3 \rightarrow H_2O + CO_2$	

What are oxidation and reduction?

oxidation [ahk-suh-DAY-shun]:   linkup of oxygen with another substance; a loss of
   electrons
reduction [ri-DUK-shun]:   separation of oxygen from a substance; a gain of
   electrons

LESSON 35 | What are oxidation and reduction?

Oxidation and reduction are opposite kinds of chemical reactions.

Oxidation [ahk-suh-DAY-shun] takes place when oxygen combines with another substance.

For example, when a flashbulb goes off, oxygen combines with aluminum.

The aluminum becomes oxidized. Aluminum oxide (Al_2O_3) forms.

$$4Al \quad + \quad 3O_2 \quad \longrightarrow \quad 2Al_2O_3$$

Aluminum   Oxygen   Aluminum oxide

Reduction [ri-DUK-shun] takes place when oxygen separates from a compound.

For example, electrolysis decomposes molten aluminum oxide (Al_2O_3). The oxygen separates from the aluminum. We say the aluminum oxide is reduced.

$$2Al_2O_3 \quad \longrightarrow \quad 4Al \quad + \quad 3O_2$$

Aluminum oxide   Aluminum   Oxygen

Here is another reduction equation. Notice what happens to the oxygen.

$$2Fe_2O_3 \quad + \quad 3C \quad \longrightarrow \quad 3CO_2 \quad + \quad 4Fe$$

Iron oxide   Carbon   Carbon dioxide   Iron

The oxygen has separated from the iron. But the oxygen is not free oxygen. It is now part of the compound carbon dioxide. It makes no difference whether a separated oxygen becomes free oxygen or part of a new compound. As long as oxygen is separated from a compound, the reaction is reduction.

Figure A   *Rusting is an example of slow oxidation.*

Figure B   *Fire is an example of rapid oxidation.*

UNDERSTANDING OXIDATION AND REDUCTION

Look at Figures C and D. Study the equations. Then answer the questions or fill in the blanks.

The burning of carbon

This equation describes what happens when carbon burns:

$$C + O_2 \longrightarrow CO_2$$

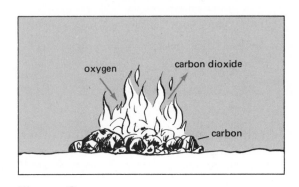

Figure C

1. Name the elements that react together when carbon burns.

   _____ _____

2. **a)** When carbon burns, oxygen _____ the carbon.
   <small>combines with, separates from</small>

   b) What product forms? _____

3. In oxidation, oxygen _____ another substance.
   <small>combines with, separates from</small>

4. In reduction, oxygen _____ a compound.
   <small>combines with, separates from</small>

5. When carbon burns, the carbon is _____ .
   <small>oxidized, reduced</small>

The electrolysis of water

The equation for the electrolysis of water is:

$$2H_2O \longrightarrow 2H_2 + O_2$$

6. Name the elements that make up water.

_____   _____

7. Electrolysis _____ water.
   forms, decomposes

8. When water decomposes, oxygen

   _____ hydrogen.
   combines with, separates from

9. The separation of oxygen from a com

   pound is called _____ .
   oxidation, reduction

10. In the electrolysis of water, the hydrogen

    is _____ .
    oxidized, reduced

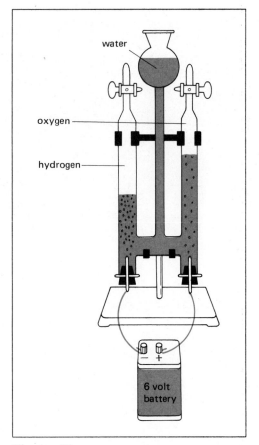

Figure D

ANOTHER VIEW OF OXIDATION AND REDUCTION

Oxidation combines oxygen with another substance.

Reduction separates oxygen from a compound.

This is true. But to a chemist, oxidation and reduction mean even more. A chemist thinks of oxidation and reduction in terms of <u>electrons lost</u> or <u>electrons gained</u>.

To a chemist,

• Oxidation means a loss of electrons.

• Reduction means a gain of electrons.

The reaction may or may not involve oxygen. This means that oxidation and reduction can happen without oxygen. All that is needed is a loss of electrons by one atom and the gain of electrons by some other atom.

Oxidation and reduction always happen together. It is easy to understand why...When one atom loses electrons, some other atom gains them.

Let us look at the burning of carbon and the electrolysis of water again. This time, look in terms of electrons gained and electrons lost.

Look at Figure E. Answer the questions or fill in the blanks.

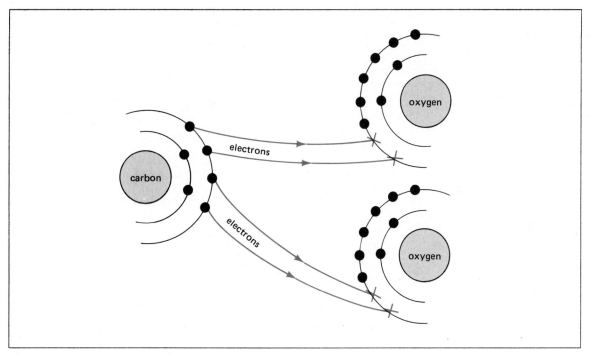

Figure E *What happens when carbon burns.*

1. When carbon burns, the carbon _____ electrons and the oxygen
   <u>lends, borrows</u>

   _____ electrons.
   <u>lends, borrows</u>

2. When carbon burns, the carbon _____ electrons and oxygen
   <u>gains, loses</u>

   _____ electrons.
   <u>gains, loses</u>

3. Oxidation is the _____ of electrons.
   <u>gain, loss</u>

4. Reduction is the _____ of electrons.
   <u>gain, loss</u>

5. When carbon burns, the carbon is _____ and the oxygen is
   <u>oxidized, reduced</u>

   _____ .
   <u>oxidized, reduced</u>

6. Oxidation and reduction happen together because electrons _____ by

   one atom are _____ by some other atom.

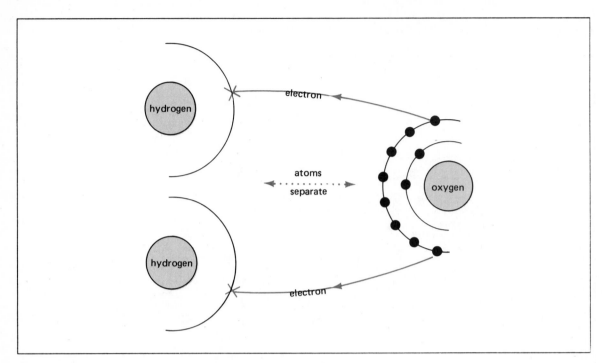

Figure F *What happens during the electrolysis of water.*

7. Electrolysis _____ water.
   _{forms, decomposes}

8. When water decomposes, electrons move from the _____ to the
   _{hydrogen, oxygen}

   _____ .
   _{hydrogen, oxygen}

9. The hydrogen _____ electrons and the oxygen _____
   _{gains, loses}   _{gains, loses}

   electrons.

10. Oxidation is the _____ of electrons.
    _{gain, loss}

11. Reduction is the _____ of electrons.
    _{gain, loss}

12. During the electrolysis of water, the hydrogen is _____ and the
    _{oxidized, reduced}

    oxygen is _____ .
    _{oxidized, reduced}

13. Why do oxidation and reduction always happen together? _____

_____

OXIDATION OR REDUCTION

Each equation listed below is either an oxidation or a reduction reaction. Which one is it? Put a check (✓) in the correct box next to each equation.

	Equation	Oxidation	Reduction
1.	$2Ba + O_2 \rightarrow 2BaO$		
2.	$2HgO \rightarrow 2Hg + O_2$		
3.	$ZnO + C \rightarrow Zn + CO$		
4.	$4Na + O_2 \rightarrow 2Na_2O$		
5.	$CuO + H_2 \rightarrow Cu + H_2O$		
6.	$N_2 + O_2 \rightarrow 2NO$		
7.	$4Ag + O_2 \rightarrow 2Ag_2O$		
8.	$SnO_2 + 2C \rightarrow Sn + 2CO$		
9.	$C + O_2 \rightarrow CO_2$		
10.	$Fe_2O_3 + 3CO \rightarrow 2Fe + 3CO_2$		

REACHING OUT

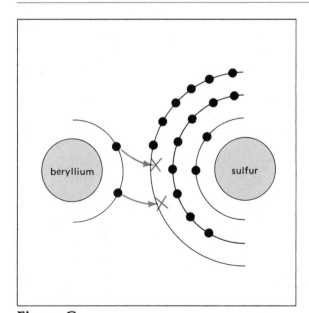

Figure G

Beryllium links up with sulfur to form beryllium sulfide.

$$\textbf{Be + S} \longrightarrow \textbf{BeS}$$

No oxygen is involved in this reaction. Yet it is an oxidation-reduction reaction.

Why is this an oxidation-reduction reaction? _____

_____

_____

SCIENCE *EXTRA*

Pharmacist

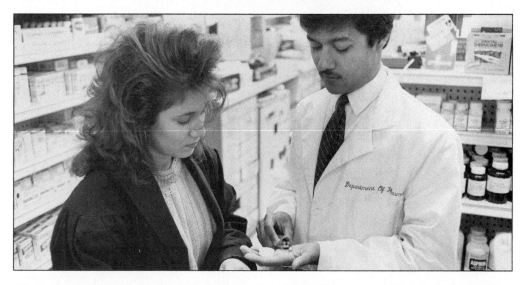

Have you ever taken a prescription drug to get better when you were sick? If you have, then you have two people to thank.

The first person is obvious — your doctor. The doctor examined you, figured out what was wrong with you, and wrote up a prescription. The second person is not as obvious but is just as important. It is your pharmacist.

A pharmacist is a person who prepares prescriptions. Pharmacists understand the chemical compositions of medicines. Therefore, they can safely mix them. Pharmacists know what medicines are safe to take together and what medicines could be harmful if used together. Pharmacists also may know what a person's allergies are and if they would have an allergic reaction to certain medications.

Pharmacists, like doctors, know a great deal about medicine and how to help people get well. Therefore,

pharmacists can help you choose non-prescription medicines. Non-prescription medicines are also called over-the-counter medicines. If you tell your pharmacist about a medical problem you are having, he or she may be able to recommend an over-the-counter remedy or suggest that you see your doctor.

Pharmacists can work in a pharmacy, drug store, or a hospital filling prescriptions. Pharmacists can also work for a company that develops medications. They work in laboratories and try to develop new and improved drugs.

As you can see, being a pharmacist is both interesting and rewarding. To become a pharmacist, you should study chemistry, biology and math in school. Pharmacists usually study for five years at a College of Pharmacy. After they graduate, students work in an internship with a pharmacist. Finally, students take a state exam to receive a license to become a pharmacist.

THE METRIC SYSTEM

METRIC-ENGLISH CONVERSIONS

	Metric to English	English to Metric
Length	1 kilometer = 0.621 mile (mi)	1 mi = 1.61 km
	1 meter = 3.28 feet (ft)	1 ft = 0.305 m
	1 centimeter = 0.394 inch (in)	1 in = 2.54 cm
Area	1 square meter = 10.763 square feet	1 ft^2 = 0.0929 m^2
	1 square centimeter = 0.155 square inch	1 in^2 = 6.452 cm^2
Volume	1 cubic meter = 35.315 cubic feet	1 ft^3 = 0.0283 m^3
	1 cubic centimeter = 0.0610 cubic inches	1 in^3 = 16.39 cm^3
	1 liter = .2642 gallon (gal)	1 gal = 3.79 L
	1 liter = 1.06 quart (qt)	1 qt = 0.94 L
Mass	1 kilogram = 2.205 pound (lb)	1 lb = 0.4536 kg
	1 gram = 0.0353 ounce (oz)	1 oz = 28.35 g
Temperature	Celsius = 5/9 (°F –32)	Fahrenheit = 9/5°C + 32
	0°C = 32°F (Freezing point of water)	72°F = 22°C (Room temperature)
	100°C = 212°F	98.6°F = 37°C
	(Boiling point of water)	(Human body temperature)

METRIC UNITS

The basic unit is printed in capital letters.

Length	Symbol
Kilometer	km
METER	m
centimeter	cm
millimeter	mm

Area	Symbol
square kilometer	km^2
SQUARE METER	m^2
square millimeter	mm^2

Volume	Symbol
CUBIC METER	m^3
cubic millimeter	mm^3
liter	L
milliliter	mL

Mass	Symbol
KILOGRAM	kg
gram	g

Temperature	Symbol
degree Celsius	°C

SOME COMMON METRIC PREFIXES

Prefix		Meaning
micro-	=	0.000001, or 1/1,000,000
milli-	=	0.001, or 1/1000
centi-	=	0.01, or 1/100
deci-	=	0.1, or 1/10
deka-	=	10
hecto-	=	100
kilo-	=	1000
mega-	=	1,000,000

SOME METRIC RELATIONSHIPS

Unit	Relationship
kilometer	1 km = 1000 m
meter	1 m = 100 cm
centimeter	1 cm = 10 mm
millimeter	1 mm = 0.1 cm
liter	1 L = 1000 mL
milliliter	1 mL = 0.001 L
tonne	1 t = 1000 kg
kilogram	1 kg = 1000 g
gram	1 g = 1000 mg
centigram	1 cg = 10 mg
milligram	1 mg = 0.001 g

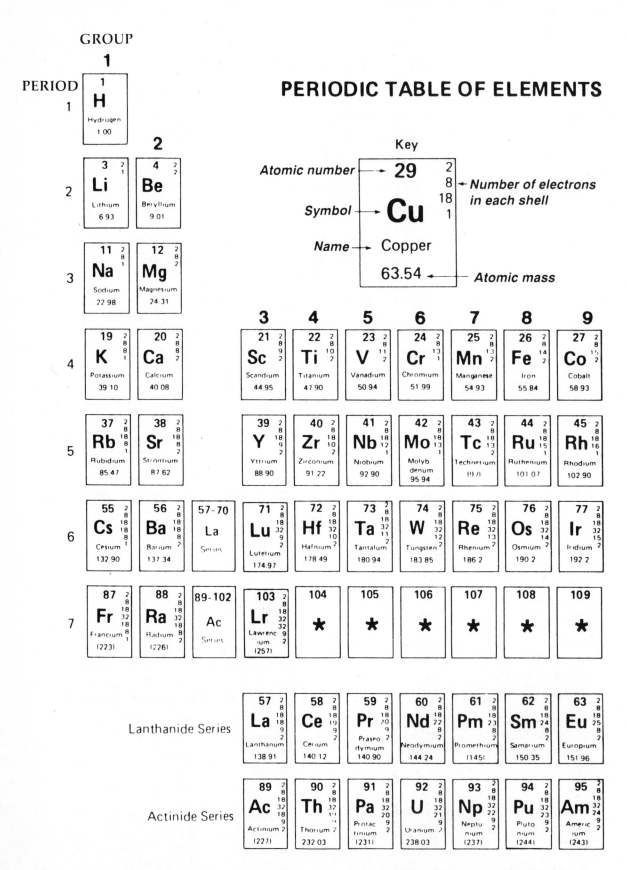

PERIODIC TABLE OF ELEMENTS

GROUP

Key

Atomic number →	**29**	2 8 ← Number of electrons
		18 in each shell
Symbol →	**Cu**	1
Name →	Copper	
	63.54 ←	— Atomic mass

* Names for these elements have not been agreed upon.

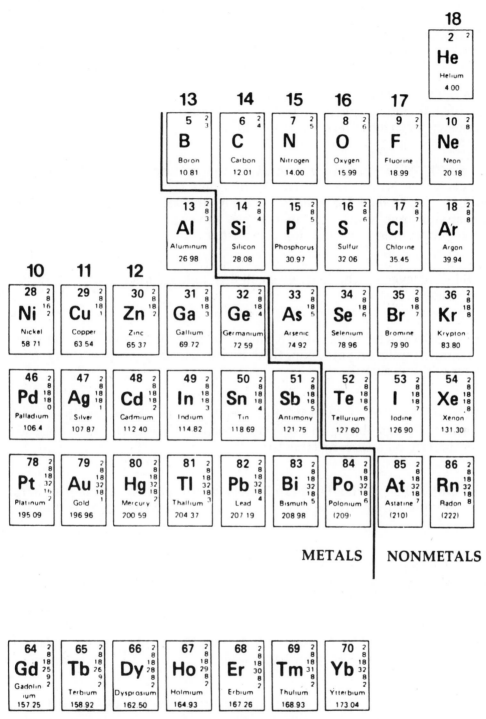

18
2 ² He Helium 4.00

13	14	15	16	17	
5 ²₃ B Boron 10.81	6 ²₄ C Carbon 12.01	7 ²₅ N Nitrogen 14.00	8 ²₆ O Oxygen 15.99	9 ²₇ F Fluorine 18.99	10 ²₈ Ne Neon 20.18
13 ²₈₃ Al Aluminum 26.98	14 ²₈₄ Si Silicon 28.08	15 ²₈₅ P Phosphorus 30.97	16 ²₈₆ S Sulfur 32.06	17 ²₈₇ Cl Chlorine 35.45	18 ²₈₈ Ar Argon 39.94

10	11	12						
28 ²₈ ₁₆ ₂ Ni Nickel 58.71	29 ²₈ ₁₈ ₁ Cu Copper 63.54	30 ²₈ ₁₈ ₂ Zn Zinc 65.37	31 ²₈ ₁₈ ₃ Ga Gallium 69.72	32 ²₈ ₁₈ ₄ Ge Germanium 72.59	33 ²₈ ₁₈ ₅ As Arsenic 74.92	34 ²₈ ₁₈ ₆ Se Selenium 78.96	35 ²₈ ₁₈ ₇ Br Bromine 79.90	36 ²₈ ₁₈ ₈ Kr Krypton 83.80
46 ²₈ ₁₈ ₁₈ ₀ Pd Palladium 106.4	47 ²₈ ₁₈ ₁₈ ₁ Ag Silver 107.87	48 ²₈ ₁₈ ₁₈ ₂ Cd Cadmium 112.40	49 ²₈ ₁₈ ₁₈ ₃ In Indium 114.82	50 ²₈ ₁₈ ₁₈ ₄ Sn Tin 118.69	51 ²₈ ₁₈ ₁₈ ₅ Sb Antimony 121.75	52 ²₈ ₁₈ ₁₈ ₆ Te Tellurium 127.60	53 ²₈ ₁₈ ₁₈ ₇ I Iodine 126.90	54 ²₈ ₁₈ ₁₈ ₈ Xe Xenon 131.30
78 ²₈ ₁₈ ₃₂ ₁₆ ₂ Pt Platinum 195.09	79 ²₈ ₁₈ ₃₂ ₁₈ ₁ Au Gold 196.96	80 ²₈ ₁₈ ₃₂ ₁₈ ₂ Hg Mercury 200.59	81 ²₈ ₁₈ ₃₂ ₁₈ ₃ Tl Thallium 204.37	82 ²₈ ₁₈ ₃₂ ₁₈ ₄ Pb Lead 207.19	83 ²₈ ₁₈ ₃₂ ₁₈ ₅ Bi Bismuth 208.98	84 ²₈ ₁₈ ₃₂ ₁₈ ₆ Po Polonium (209)	85 ²₈ ₁₈ ₃₂ ₁₈ ₇ At Astatine (210)	86 ²₈ ₁₈ ₃₂ ₁₈ ₈ Rn Radon (222)

METALS | NONMETALS

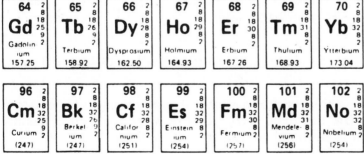

64 ²₈ ₁₈ ₂₅ ₉ ₂ Gd Gadolinium 157.25	65 ²₈ ₁₈ ₂₆ ₉ ₂ Tb Terbium 158.92	66 ²₈ ₁₈ ₂₈ ₈ ₂ Dy Dysprosium 162.50	67 ²₈ ₁₈ ₂₉ ₈ ₂ Ho Holmium 164.93	68 ²₈ ₁₈ ₃₀ ₈ ₂ Er Erbium 167.26	69 ²₈ ₁₈ ₃₁ ₈ ₂ Tm Thulium 168.93	70 ²₈ ₁₈ ₃₂ ₈ ₂ Yb Ytterbium 173.04
96 ²₈ ₁₈ ₃₂ ₂₅ ₉ ₂ Cm Curium (247)	97 ²₈ ₁₈ ₃₂ ₂₆ ₉ ₂ Bk Berkelium (247)	98 ²₈ ₁₈ ₃₂ ₂₈ ₈ ₂ Cf Californium (251)	99 ²₈ ₁₈ ₃₂ ₂₉ ₈ ₂ Es Einsteinium (254)	100 ²₈ ₁₈ ₃₂ ₃₀ ₈ ₂ Fm Fermium (257)	101 ²₈ ₁₈ ₃₂ ₃₁ ₈ ₂ Md Mendelevium (256)	102 ²₈ ₁₈ ₃₂ ₃₂ ₈ ₂ No Nobelium (254)

SAFETY ALERT SYMBOLS

 CLOTHING PROTECTION • A lab coat protects clothing from stains. • Always confine loose clothing.

 EYE SAFETY • Always wear safety goggles. • If anything gets in your eyes, flush them with plenty of water. • Be sure you know how to use the emergency wash system in the laboratory.

 FIRE SAFETY • Never get closer to an open flame than is necessary. • Never reach across an open flame. • Confine loose clothing. • Tie back loose hair. • Know the location of the fire-extinguisher and fire blanket. • Turn off gas valves when not in use. • Use proper procedures when lighting any burner.

 POISON • Never touch, taste, or smell any unknown substance. Wait for your teacher's instruction.

 CAUSTIC SUBSTANCES • Some chemicals can irritate and burn the skin. If a chemical spills on your skin, flush it with plenty of water. Notify your teacher without delay.

 HEATING SAFETY • Handle hot objects with tongs or insulated gloves. • Put hot objects on a special lab surface or on a heat-resistant pad; never directly on a desk or table top.

 SHARP OBJECTS • Handle sharp objects carefully. • Never point a sharp object at yourself, or anyone else. • Cut in the direction away from your body.

 TOXIC VAPORS • Some vapors (gases) can injure the skin, eyes, and lungs. Never inhale vapors directly. • Use your hand to "wave" a small amount of vapor towards your nose.

 GLASSWARE SAFETY • Never use broken or chipped glassware. • Never pick up broken glass with your bare hands.

 CLEAN UP • Wash your hands thoroughly after any laboratory activity.

 ELECTRICAL SAFETY • Never use an electrical appliance near water or on a wet surface. • Do not use wires if the wire covering seems worn. • Never handle electrical equipment with wet hands.

 DISPOSAL • Discard all materials properly according to your teacher's directions.

GLOSSARY/INDEX

absorb: take in, 28

acid: substance that reacts with metals to release hydrogen, 144

base: substance formed when metals react with water, 150

borrow: to use something that belongs to someone or something else, 58

calorie [KAL-uh-ree]: unit used to measure heat, 34

Celsius [SEL-see-us]: metric temperature scale, 40

chemical change: change in matter that produces new substances, 66, 190

chemical equation: set of symbols and formulas that describe a chemical change, 190

chemical formula: short way of writing a compound, 52

chemical reaction: process involving a chemical change, 66

coagulation [koh-ag-yoo-LAY-shun]: use of chemicals to make the particles in a suspension clump together, 98

coefficient [koh-uh-FISH-unt]: number that shows how many molecules of a substance are involved in a chemical reaction, 187

colloids [KAHL-oydz]: suspension in which the particles are permanently suspended, 95

compound: matter made up of two or more different elements, 46

concentrated [KAHN-sun-trayt-ed] **solution:** strong solution, 118

condensation [kahn-dun-SAY-shun]: change of a gas to a liquid, 138

conduction [kun-DUK-shun]: way heat moves through solids, 16

conductors: substances that conduct heat easily, 16

contract: make smaller, 8

convection [kuhn-VEK-shun]: way heat moves through liquids and gases, 22

decomposition [dee-kahm-puh-ZISH-un]: breakdown of a substance into simpler substances, 210

degree: unit used to measure temperature, 34

dilute: [di-LEWT] **solution:** weak solution, 118

dissolve: go into solution, to make a solid matter disappear in a liquid, 82, 106

distillationn [dis-tuh-LAY-shun]: process of evaporating a liquid and then condensing the gas back into a liquid, 138

electrolysis [i-lek-TRAHL-uh-sis]: decomposition of a substance by means of electricity, 210

electrolyte [i-LEK-truh-lyt]: substance that conducts an electric current when it is dissolved in water, 162

emulsions [i-MUL-shunz]: suspension of two liquids, 90

evaporate [i-VAP-uh-rayt]: change from a liquid to a gas, 82

evaporation [i-vap-uh-RAY-shun]: change of a liquid to a gas at the surface of the liquid, 138

expand: make larger, 8

Fahrenheit [FER-un-hyt]: temperature scale, 40

filtration [fil-TRAY-shun]: separation of particles in a suspension by passing it through paper or other substances, 98

formula mass: sum of the mass numbers of all atoms in a molecule, 184

friction: force that opposes the motion of an object, 2

heat: form of energy in moving particles of matter, 2

homogeneous [hoh-muh-JEE-nee-us]: uniform; the same all the way through, 112

indicator [IN-duh-kayt-ur]: substance that changes color in acids and bases, 144

inert gases: elements which have complete outer electron shells, gases which rarely react with other elements, 63

insulators: substances that do not conduct heat easily, 16

ion [Y-un]: charged particle, 162

Law of Conservation of Matter: scientific statement that says that a chemical reaction does not destroy or create matter, 196

lend: to let someone use something that belongs to you, 58

mixture: two or more substances that are physically combined, 74

molecule [MAHL-uh-kyool]: the smallest part of a compound that has all the properties of that compound, two or more atoms linked together, 46

neutral: neither acidic nor basic, 156

neutralization [new-truh-li-ZAY-shun]: reaction between an acid and a base to produce a salt and water, 156

noble gases: inert gases, 63

oxidation [ahk-suh-DAY-shun]: linkup of oxygen with another substance; a loss of electrons, 222

oxidation numbers: how many electrons an atom can lend or borrow, 168

phenolphthalein [fee-nohl-THAL-een]: an indicator that turns a deep pink color when a base is added, 150

physical change: a change in matter that does not produce any new products or substances, 66, 190

polyatomic [PAHL-i-uh-tahm-ik] **ion:** group of atoms that acts as a single atom, 176

polyvalent [pahl-i-VAY-lunt]: having more than one oxidation number, 180

product: a substance that is produced in a chemical reaction (change), 190

properties: [PROP-ur-tees]: characteristics used to describe a substance, 112

radiation [ray-dee-AY-shun]: the way heat moves through empty space, 28

reactant: substance that takes part in a chemical reaction (change), 190

reduction [ri-DUK-shun]: separation of oxygen from a substance; a gain of electrons, 222

reflect: bounce off, 28

replacement: reaction in which one kind of matter replaces another kind, 216

saturated [SACH-uh-rayt-id] **solution:** solution containing all the solute it can hold at a given temperature, 118

shells: energy levels in which electrons are arranged around the nucleus, 58

solute [SAHL-yoot]: substance that is dissolved in a solvent, 106

solution: mixture in which one substance is evenly mixed with another substance, 106

solvent: substance in which a solute dissolves, 106

stable: is not likely to change, prefers to stay the way it is, 58

subscript: number written to the lower right of a chemical symbol, 176

suspensions [suh-SPEN-shun]: cloudy mixture of two or more substances that settle on standing, 90

synthesis [SIN-thuh-sis] **reaction:** combining of several substances to form a more complicated substance, 204

temperature: measure of how hot or cold something is, 34

thermometer: instrument to measure temperature, 34

transparent [trans-PER-unt]: material that transmits light easily, 112

Tyndall effect: scattering of a light beam by particles in a colloid, 93